The Stage Directions
Guide to
Musical Theater

Heinemann's STAGE DIRECTIONS Series

The Stage Directions Guide to Musical Theater

Edited by

Stephen Peithman

Neil Offen

HEINEMANN
Portsmouth, NH

HEINEMANN
A division of Reed Elsevier Inc.
361 Hanover Street
Portsmouth, NH 03801–3912
www.heinemanndrama.com

Offices and agents throughout the world

The editors and publisher wish to thank those who have generously given permission to reprint borrowed material:

Lyric excerpts of "Lonely Room" and "The Surrey With The Fringe On Top" by Richard Rodgers and Oscar Hammerstein II. Copyright © 1943 by Williamson Music. Copyright Renewed. International Copyright Secured. Reprinted by Permission. All Rights Reserved.

Lyric excerpt from "Sunday in the Park with George" by Stephen Sondheim. All Rights Reserved. Used by Permission of Warner Bros. Publications U. S. Inc., Miami, FL 33014

LIBRARY OF CONGRESS CATALOGING-IN-PUBLICATION DATA
The Stage directions guide to musical theater / edited by Stephen
    Peithman and Neil Offen.
        p.   cm.—(Heinemann's Stage directions series)
    Includes bibliographical references and videography.
    ISBN 0-325-00349-1 (alk. paper)
        1. Musical theater—Production and direction.   I. Title: Guide to
    musical theater.   II. Peithman, Stephen.   III. Offen, Neil.
    IV. Stage directions.   V. Series.

    MT955 .S69 2001
    792.6'0233—dc21

                                                              2001039906

Editor: Lisa A. Barnett
Production: Abigail M. Heim
Cover design: Barbara Werden
Cover photograph: Copyright, 2001, Rob Karosis
Manufacturing: Steve Bernier

Printed in the United States of America on acid-free paper

05   04   03   02   01   VP   1   2   3   4   5

*For all those in front of the lights and behind the scenes
who understand the magic of theater*

Contents

Foreword

For many people, it is their first glimpse of live theater—in school, at a local community theater, in a professional performance by a national touring company, or, perhaps most fortunate of all, in a big Broadway house. For others, musical theater is a form of entertainment they seek out often, on any or all of the stages mentioned.

But for still others, it is much more. For them, active participation in musical theater is a way they can exercise their creative vision and their varied talents as directors, actors, designers, and musicians. And it is for them that this book was written.

Musical theater has evolved over four hundred years and today, despite many changes, it is as popular with theatergoers as ever. What is the source of its strength?

Certainly, one reason is that it is total theater. It encompasses spoken dialogue, song, dance, and instrumental music; yet, it is greater than the sum of those parts. In a well-written musical, a song serves as more than mere entertainment. It can tell us the inner thoughts of a character, for example, or further the plot. A well-choreographed dance number in a musical can heighten the excitement or provide insight into motivation.

Musical theater also is democratic theater, a form of entertainment created by and for the majority of people. Of course, tastes change over time—opera, operetta, and comic opera all were "popular" forms of entertainment at one time. And although it must be acknowledged that the future of American musical theater is cloudy, at present it remains firmly embedded in popular culture.

Finally, and more important from the perspective of the participant, musical theater is the most collaborative of the performing arts, blending the skills of composer, lyricist, librettist, director, choreographer, actors, singers, dancers, conductor, music director, instrumentalists, and designers of costumes, lighting, and sets. This interdependence creates challenges and rewards at every turn.

To examine these challenges and help reap the rewards, in *The Stage Directions Guide to Musical Theater* we have blended our own knowledge and experience in this area with the expertise of veteran directors, choreographers, musical directors, and performers in community, regional, and academic theater. After an overview of the essential elements of musical theater, the book focuses on five main areas of responsibility: producing, directing, musical direction, performance, and technical support.

While much of this book is geared toward directors, a great deal of the information is helpful for performers as well. This is particularly true of the sections on the elements of the musical ("Putting It Together," Chapter 2) and the comments on character development ("I'm the Greatest Star," Chapter 28). Also, although we cover some aspects of auditions, directors and actors will find additional help in *The Stage Directions Guide to Auditions*. Directors also will find much valuable information of a general nature in *The Stage Directions Guide to Directing*.

Whether you are a veteran of many productions or a newcomer to the stage, we hope *The Stage Directions Guide to Musical Theater* provides you with the tools you need to unlock the potential of your production and performance in this enduring art form.

About Stage Directions *and This Book*

Much of the material in this book is based on information that first appeared in the pages of *Stage Directions*, the "practical magazine of theater." Since 1988, *Stage Directions* has published articles on a wide variety of subject matter—not only acting and directing, but also management, publicity, scenic and costume design, lighting and special effects, and much more.

During that time, we've taken a close look at almost every aspect of musical theater. We've put all that advice together in this book, updated and revised as needed, and added introductions that help put the information into perspective.

As we do with the magazine, we'd like to hear your comments on this book or suggestions for future topics in our expanding library of *Stage Directions* books. Please write to us c/o Heinemann, 361 Hanover Street, Portsmouth, NH 03801-3912.

Stephen Peithman
Neil Offen

Introduction

*P*erhaps the greatest challenge in producing, directing, or performing in a musical is creating an illusion
of reality in what is perhaps the least realistic of all
theater forms. Somehow, our efforts must produce in
the audience what Samuel Taylor Coleridge called "the willing
suspension of disbelief for the moment."

In other words, during the time that the story is played out
on stage, the audience must accept what it sees as "real,"
despite the fact that—unlike real life—characters express their
thoughts and feelings in song and dance, as well as in speech.

The suspension of disbelief is a fragile construct, however.
Musicals have their own reality, which is different from the
reality of the nonmusical play—just as both are different from
the reality of the outside world.

It is the job of the director, musical director, designers,
choreographer, and performers to create this reality. And, as
Stephen Sondheim has written, "Art isn't easy."

That's particularly true in musical theater, where there are
so many separate elements that must be woven into a seamless
whole; more than song and dance are involved here. As Aaron
Frankel notes in *Writing the Broadway Musical* (Drama Book
Publishers), "a musical has an inner music and an inner movement that anticipate song and dance. It has an orchestration of

all its elements to be divined, a rhythm to be sensed. There is an encompassing vision to bring to it. If the writers imagine, so will the audience."

It is the job of those who present the musical in performance to help make clear the writers' vision to the audience, even as the director and performers bring their own vision to the mix as well. It's a journey of discovery.

So, let's begin it.

*The Stage Directions
Guide to
Musical Theater*

THE WHAT AND HOW
OF MUSICAL THEATER
Understanding
the Basics

*B*efore we can create a musical, we have to understand the basic elements of musical theater style.
Let's start, then, by reviewing those basic elements,
which guide all aspects of a production. An understanding of these elements will help you create a memorable
experience for your audiences.

1 | "I Got a Song"

The Forms of Musical Theater

While it may seem straightforward, the term *musical theater* actually covers a large territory—grand opera, comic opera, operetta, vaudeville, revue, musical comedy, and musical play. All involve a series of musical numbers, often interspersed with dialogue (spoken or sung), performed on a stage in front of an audience. And yet, *La Boheme* is a very different creation than *Rent*, even though they share the same basic story line. Even among the ranks of modern Broadway musicals, there are differences—sometimes subtle, sometimes blatant.

However, as Richard Kislan points out in *The Musical: A Look at the American Musical Theater* (Applause Books), all musical theater is essentially presentational. In other words, musical performance openly acknowledges the presence of the audience. This is quite different than much of nonmusical theater, in which audience members observe the onstage action without the knowledge of the characters. This is the theatrical concept of the *fourth wall*, which refers to the proscenium as a one-way glass partition that allows us to eavesdrop on the characters' lives.

In musical theater, the fourth wall is transparent on both sides. In fact, it often disappears completely.

"The cumulative impact of live singing, dancing, acting, and musical accompaniment reminds the audience and the performers throughout of the vigorous theatricality of the event," Kislan writes. "A musical not only welcomes a spontaneous and displayed audience reaction, but builds for it, thrives on it, and learns from it."

However, while all musical theater is presentational, the presentation itself takes on a multiplicity of forms. Some understanding of this fact is key to the success of your production, so here's a brief overview of the styles found on the musical stage.

Opera

The oldest form of musical theater still produced with any regularity is opera—sometimes called *grand opera* to distinguish it from *comic* or *light opera* (following). *Opera* can be defined as a heavily dramatic work in which most or all of the dialogue is sung. Typically, it demands trained voices that can sustain long melodic phrases, often with considerable volume. Because operas such as *La Boheme, Carmen*, and *Madame Butterfly* call for big voices, full orchestra, large casts, and extensive sets and costumes, they are most often performed by large professional companies. Operas are also produced by small companies (often with piano accompaniment, minimal sets, and costumes); however, while production values can be trimmed, the vocal demands of the music still must be met. Thus, unless there is a supply of accomplished singers, traditional opera is usually beyond the range of community-theater companies.

Comic Opera

The subject matter of grand opera is heavily dramatic. *Comic opera*, however, is a work with a large amount of music, on a light or humorous subject, with a happy ending, and in which comic elements play a significant role. A product of the middle to late nineteenth century, the music of comic opera is almost always more "popular" in style than that of serious opera of the same era, generally easier both to perform and to comprehend, and appealing to less sophisticated audiences. For example, the vocal demands of Gilbert and Sullivan's works (*The Mikado, The Pirates of Penzance*) are not as great as opera, although the lead roles normally require trained voices. However, the large amount of spoken dialogue also means that performers must be able to deliver in that mode as well.

European Operetta or Light Opera

The terms *light opera* and *operetta* are often used interchangeably, and *light opera* has been used to label everything from *The Merry Widow* to *My Fair Lady*. To add to the confusion, American operetta is different than European operetta, which originated in Vienna with such composers as Von Suppe, and in Paris with Jacques Offenbach. Vienna reigned as the capital of operetta with the works of Johann Strauss, Jr., and Franz Lehar. Their operettas are generally comic and sophisticated, and include spoken dialogue. Examples of European operetta still produced today include Strauss's *Die Fleidermaus* and Lehar's *The Merry Widow*, as well as Offenbach's *La Perichole* and *Orpheus in the Underworld*.

American Operetta

In this country, operetta took a very different turn. Stories tended toward the exotic, sentimental, and heavily romantic, and comedy was relegated to secondary characters. Examples include *Naughty Marietta, The New Moon, The Student Prince*, and *The Desert Song*. Jerome Kern's *Show Boat* is in the operetta tradition, but also marks the early stages of what later came to be known as the *musical play* (described later).

Revue

In essence, a *revue* is a series of musical numbers and sketches, sometimes (but not always) with music by the same composer and lyricist, and most often built around a unifying theme. However, there is no plot, and even if there are continuing characters (as in *You're a Good Man, Charlie Brown*), they do not develop or change.

The revue originated in France, but took on a life of its own in America, where *The Ziegfeld Follies* was an early example, with many extravagant editions between 1907 and 1936 (as well as some later, unfortunate attempts to revive it). Beginning in the 1930s, however, revues tended toward more intimate staging, allowing a small cast to show off their talents. Examples include *The Band Wagon, As Thousands Cheer*, and *Pins and Needles*. In recent decades, revues have become among the most produced form of musical theater on and off Broadway. Productions such as *Ain't Misbehavin'* and *Putting It Together* saluted an individual composer, while *Tintypes* and *Swing!* evoked an era, using songs by many different writers. Some revues, such as *Cats, Hair*, and *Pump Boys and Dinettes*, present continuing characters and situations, even while they do not actually have a plot in the conventional sense.

Musical Comedy

A *musical comedy* combines music, dance, and dialogue to tell a story that employs farfetched situations and exaggerated or even two-dimensional characters. The music is decidedly "popular" in style (in whatever way "pop" music is defined at that moment), and the songs may or may not be tied closely to the plot or characters. Classic examples include *Anything Goes* and *Babes in Arms* from the 1930s, but more recent shows, such as *Annie* and *How to Succeed in Business Without Really Trying*, carry on the tradition.

Musical Play

Rodgers and Hammerstein are credited with fully developing (and naming) this form, which blends musical comedy and operetta—although Jerome Kern and Oscar Hammerstein's *Show Boat* predates *Oklahoma!* by sixteen years. In general, the musical play aims at something more serious than operetta or musical comedy.

Sometimes it is the show's theme that is serious—*Show Boat* and *South Pacific* both deal with racism, for example. But more important is Hammerstein's dictum that musical numbers must serve the book—a seriousness of purpose marked by both sincerity and enthusiasm. Before Hammerstein, musicals were free to place songs anywhere—and often did so with the flimsiest of excuses ("Say, did I ever sing you that song my mother sang to me?"). But with Hammerstein, the story—the *book* in musical-theater parlance—came first. Songs set the scene ("Oh, What a Beautiful Mornin'," "The Sound of Music"), furthered the plot ("The Farmer and the Cowman," "Shall We Dance?," "Climb Ev'ry Mountain"), or illuminated a character's inner feelings ("Hello, Young Lovers," "Out of My Dreams," "Twin Soliloquies"). This was an important advance, and after *Oklahoma!* in 1943, musicals that did not wed songs to story often were dismissed by the critics.

Concept Musical

A production in which the total presentation is more important than any one part—including the book—is called a *concept musical*. It is an inexact term, but normally is the work of a strong director/choreographer who impresses his or her centralized vision on everything in the show. Thus, *A Chorus Line* is called a concept musical because the look of the show is essential to its success. That's why it is seldom performed any other way than the original—bare stage, rehearsal costumes. *Chicago* and *Pippin,* as conceived on Broadway, are concept shows as well for, in both, the plot is subordinate to the choreographic presentation.

Understanding the basic style of a musical is important. It would be foolish to present *The King and I* in the same way you might present *Annie,* for example. Each is a classic musical, and yet each calls for a very different approach. *The King and I* is a musical play in which issues of life and death play a central role, even while entertaining us with song and dance. *Annie* is also a song-and-dance show, but it presents a cartoon world in which the good are rewarded and the wicked are punished. When done well, these shows produce strong feelings of enjoyment, but for very different reasons.

In the next chapter, we look at how those feelings are produced.

"Putting It Together" 2

What Makes a Musical Work

*T*he modern musical is a combination of a book (the dialogue and story) and the score (music and lyrics). But it's not as simple as putting these two elements together—if it were, there would be many more masterpieces of musical theater.

It's rather like building a house. Almost anyone can gather all the building materials needed for construction. Fewer people have the skill to figure out how all the pieces go together. And fewer still have the creative talent to design an architectural work of art.

Luckily, most of us in the theater are working from an architect's blueprint—the book and score. But, taking our analogy a step farther, some of us are better than others at turning that blueprint into a first-rate production. The difference is usually a matter of understanding the basics of construction—whether we're talking about a house or a musical.

The Score

The *score* of a musical refers to the music, which may be sung or played or danced to (or all three). For the purpose of telling the story or building character, however, the song is most important.

Musical-theater songs typically are constructed to include a verse and a chorus. The verse sets up the premise of a song and can be of most any length. For example, in *Oklahoma!*, "The Surrey with the Fringe on Top" begins with a verse, the first words of which are "When I take you out tonight with me," and ends with "In the slickest gig you ever see!" This sets up the chorus, which begins with the words "Chicks and ducks and geese better scurry."

When a theater song is sung by a popular artist outside the context of the show, the verse often is dropped. This allows the singer to get to the main tune (the chorus) more quickly, of course, but there's another reason. Typically, the verse deals with subjects that are specific to the character and situation in the show, and thus need special attention from both director and performer.

The *chorus* of a song states the main point of the lyric and is traditionally thirty-two bars (i.e., measures) long, divided into four sections of eight bars each, called the *AABA form*. Now, this may sound like so much academic mumbo-jumbo, but the AABA form was first developed by American musical theater and is fundamental to most of the great theater composers.

Here's how it works. "A" is the main melody, repeated three times, so that it can be easily remembered; "B" is the "release" or "bridge." The release is written to contrast with "A" and yet lead inevitably to the final repetition of the main tune.

Here's how the AABA form works in "The Surrey with the Fringe on Top," with the beginning words of each section indicated:

A: "Chicks and ducks and geese better scurry."
A: "Watch that fringe and see how it flutters."
B: "The wheels are yellow, the upholstery's brown."
A: "Two bright sidelights, winkin' and blinkin'."

If you examine your favorite show tunes, you will find this format used again and again. In fact, because of its use in musical theater, AABA became the standard for all popular music until rock and rhythm and blues became dominant in the 1960s.

In some cases, a song may double the number of bars (four sections of sixteen each), but the AABA structure and proportions remain. This forces composers and lyricists to make their points efficiently, acting more as a discipline than a limitation.

Understanding this method of song construction helps both the director and the performer. When you approach a verse as a way to particularize the song to the specific character and moment in the show, then you can allow it to develop on its own terms, rather than as "that thing you have to sing before you get to the part that everybody knows." In the same way, a performer who understands the function of the release—or "B" section of a song—can relax into it, without rushing it, so that the return to the main tune at the end comes as a pleasant homecoming for both singer and audience.

Song Types

Musical-theater songs can serve almost any dramatic purpose, but the following are most common:

Ballad. Most often a love song ("People Will Say We're in Love"), a ballad actually can express any strong emotion ("The Music of the Night," "Mama Look Sharp," "I Believe in You"). Ballads tend to be slow or mid-tempo and are often used to heighten the drama of a scene. They typically rely on a strong voice ("Some Enchanted Evening"), strong acting ability ("Send in the Clowns"), or both ("Don't Cry for Me, Argentina").

Charm Song. As the name suggests, this allows a character to beguile an audience ("The Lusty Month of May") or to set a scene ("June Is Bustin' out All Over"). Charm songs do not deal in heavy emotion, nor do they propel the plot. However, they can give us a glimpse of a character's personality or inner thoughts ("Wouldn't It Be Loverly?").

Comedy Number. Comedy songs are meant to get laughs, but do so in different ways. "Comedy Tonight" (*A Funny Thing Happened on the Way to the Forum*) sets up the entire show. "You Can't Get a Man with a Gun" (*Annie Get Your Gun*) and "One Hundred Easy Ways" (*Wonderful Town*) illuminate the lead female's frustration in attracting a lover. "You Must Meet My Wife" (*A Little Night Music*) and "Show Me" (*My Fair Lady*) help further the plot.

Musical Scene. A legacy of operetta, this blends dialogue and song in an extended sequence that may set up a dramatic confronta-tion (*A Little Night Music*'s "A Weekend in the Country") or resolve one (the finale of *Of Thee I Sing*).

Song Placement

Songs must be carefully planned for emotional high points where dia-logue is no longer enough and characters have to sing. When Dolly Levi comes down the stairs at the Harmonia Gardens, she and the waiters sing "Hello Dolly!" to express their pent-up emotions. (Having the maitre d' simply say "It's so nice to have you back" might be more realistic, but would hardly have the same impact.)

As a rule, the composer and lyricist work closely with the book-writer to plan song placement. Three spots are of particular impor-tance in most musicals:

1. The opening number sets the tone for the show—so much so that it is frequently written after the rest of a show is in place. Two great stories about opening numbers illustrate this, and both involve direc-tor/choreographer Jerome Robbins.

In its early out-of-town tryouts, *A Funny Thing Happened on the Way to the Forum* was not doing well. Puzzled, the producers called in

Robbins to have a look and listen. He watched the show, then told them that the problem was that the show opened with a song called "Love Is in the Air," which left audiences expecting a romantic comedy. It took them half of the first act to adjust to the raucous farce that followed. "You need to tell them what the show's about," he said. Stephen Sondheim wrote a new opening number—"Comedy Tonight"—and the entire show got a better reception.

Similarly, while *Fiddler on the Roof* was still on the drawing board, Robbins felt instinctively that something was missing. There was, again, nothing to tell the audience what *Fiddler* was about. He noted that the show was about "the dissolution of a way of life," and so the musical needed to begin by showing the way of life that would soon be gone; thus, the song "Tradition" was born.

2. The 11 o'clock number takes place a little past the midpoint of Act II—thus, the name. (Broadway curtain times are earlier now, so the song comes earlier as well.) Its purpose is to energize the audience for the final climactic scenes of a show, or give the star one final big moment. The typical 11 o'clock number is an up-tempo or brassy song, such as "Brush Up Your Shakespeare" (*Kiss Me, Kate*) or "Sit down, You're Rocking the Boat" (*Guys and Dolls*), but it also can be a strong ballad like *South Pacific*'s "This Nearly Was Mine," a dramatic solo number such as "Rose's Turn" (*Gypsy*), a comic number like "I'm Going Back" (*Bells Are Ringing*), or a full-fledged choral production number like "The Brotherhood of Man" (*How to Succeed in Business Without Really Trying*) or the title song of *Oklahoma!*

3. The finale ties up the package, helping the audience come full circle to a satisfying conclusion. Typically, the finale reprises (repeats) a song or songs heard earlier, sometimes with slightly different lyrics. For example, in *A Little Night Music*, Desiree sings "Send in the Clowns," a self-mocking tribute to her failed attempt to win back Fredrik. Then, at the end of the show, both characters sing the song to indicate that they have both been fools—and have a common bond.

At its best, a reprise is more than a mere repeat; the song takes on a new or deeper meaning because of what has happened since the song was sung last. This may be signaled with a slightly changed lyric. In the finale of *Oklahoma!*, Laurey and Curley sing "Let people say we're in love," for example. Sometimes the words are the same, but the feeling is different because of events that have transpired. Sometimes, it's a matter of bringing everything back full circle, as in *Chicago*'s "All That Jazz." *A Chorus Line* brings back all the dancers with a reprise of "One," while *Les Miserables* brings back the ghosts of the past for an encore of "Do You Hear the People Sing?" *Carousel* reprises "You'll Never Walk Alone" and *The Music Man* "Seventy-Six Trombones." And some musicals merely repeat a few of the big songs (sung by the chorus) while the principals take their bows, as in *Hello, Dolly!* and *Mame.*

The Book

The book or libretto is the least appreciated—but most dramatically important—element of a musical. It is the narrative structure that keeps the show from being nothing more than a medley of songs. When musicals fail, the problem almost always lies in the book. A musical with a great score but a bad book is usually doomed to failure, while one with a mediocre score and a solid book has a chance of success. After all, the first job of any theater piece is to tell a good story.

From the 1920s through the early 1940s, the books of most Broadway musicals were little more than a series of jokes and sight gags designed to get from song to song (*Show Boat* and *Of Thee I Sing* are two exceptions). By the 1940s, shows like *Pal Joey, Lady in the Dark,* and *Oklahoma!* found ways for the book and score to serve the dramatic needs of a story. Rodgers and Hammerstein dubbed this type of show the *musical play,* thus acknowledging the libretto as central to the work.

But a musical play is not simply a play with music. The demands on the libretto are many—which is one reason that it's difficult to write a good one. A musical book must keep the story line clear and easy to follow, create characters the audience will care about, develop situations that motivate those characters to sing, move smoothly into songs, and allow songs to handle as much plot and character development as possible. This is an enormous challenge because at least 50 percent of a musical's running time is taken up with musical numbers.

The modern musical libretto is almost always written in two acts. If nothing else, the intermission forces bookwriters to make sure the story has reached a dramatic point that will encourage the audience to return. The first act does not have to end with a cliff-hanger, but we should be anxious to see what happens next. In *Oklahoma!,* the first act ends with the troubling psychological drama of Laurey's dream ballet. In *Fiddler on the Roof,* we wonder how Tevye and his family will carry on after the police pogrom has ruined Tzeitel's wedding. In *My Fair Lady,* we want to find out how Eliza has done at the ball. Occasionally, a show breaks the mold: *Man of La Mancha,* for example, was written to be performed without intermission.

Final Thoughts

We've taken apart the musical, but as with most creations, the whole is greater than the sum of its parts. Otherwise, musical theater would indeed be nothing more than "a play with music."

As Stephen Sondheim writes in *Sunday in the Park with George*:

> Every moment makes a contribution,
> Every little detail plays a part.

PRODUCING THE MUSICAL

How to Choose the Right Show the Right Way

*I*n many theater companies, the choice of which shows to produce belongs to the director. In others, however, the choice is made by an artistic director or the board of directors, often with input from a committee.

Whatever your situation, choosing the right show for your situation and your company is imperative for the artistic and financial success of the production. Fortunately, as you'll learn in this section, a little research and preparation can make the process surprisingly smooth.

3 | *Thirteen Questions to Help You Focus*

hen a production goes well, praise usually goes to the acting, singing, dancing, directing, scenic design, or costumes. All these are important, of course, but the reason they stand out is that the show itself matches the performing group's capabilities.

Sometimes, finding the right musical is fortuitous. But more often, it's a case of careful thought. Here are thirteen questions to help you focus on what's right for your situation:

1. *Is it good?* This may sound elementary, but people choose plays for all sorts of reasons, not simply the quality of the work. But for a good production, the script must provide a strong story, memorable music, interesting characters, an important theme or entertaining approach, and that intangible "something" that makes a show intriguing to watch.

2. *Is the show appropriate for your audience?* Consider who is likely to attend. Will they understand the show? Will they approve of its message or language? Or will the show try to reshape their attitudes? Controversy in and of itself is not a good reason for selecting a play. You want to stir your audience, of course, but not necessarily offend them. After all, you do want them to return. *Kiss of the Spider Woman* is not appropriate for children; *Snoopy!* is. *You're a Good Man, Charlie Brown* has levels of meaning that make it appeal to both

youngsters and adults. Some shows are so familiar that directors forget they contain subject matter that some might find objectionable when played by high school students. For example, one of the characters in *Oklahoma!* is a sexually troubled man just this side of psychopathic; in *South Pacific*, a mother encourages a young lieutenant to have a sexual liaison with her daughter.

3. *Can you cast the show?* Consider not only individual actors who might take roles if offered, but also whether the percentage of males and females reflects your group or the pool of actors available to you. If you have a preponderance of women, you would be wiser to choose *The Sound of Music* than *1776*. Does the play depend on one major role played brilliantly? *Mame* or *Hello, Dolly!* each depends on one strong female lead, while *Guys and Dolls* and *Into the Woods* are ensemble shows. Which type of musical is best for you?

4. *Do you have the singers?* Some shows demand strong voices from everyone, some only from a few. Ruth, in *Wonderful Town*, for example, was written for Rosalind Russell, who admitted that she had only five notes; the part of her sister Eileen was written for Juilliard-trained Edie Adams. And it's not always a matter of a good voice, but a voice comfortable in the range of the part as written. Rosalind Russell was practically a tenor; Carol Channing certainly was. Check over the music carefully to see if the lead roles match the voice range and style of your potential performers. (Some publishers offer scores in more compatible keys; Music Theatre International even offers customized key changes for a fee.)

5. *Can you handle the instrumental requirements?* Some shows can be done with a piano, bass, and percussion—or even two pianos; others need a bigger sound. *Hello, Dolly!*'s big number, "Until the Parade Passes By," loses punch without brass and wind instruments. In fact, any show with big musical moments tends to suffer without the weight of a pit orchestra. How difficult is the music, and how much of it is there? And we're not talking just about songs; many shows have large amounts of underscoring and dance routines. Do you have musicians able to learn the music and enough time to rehearse them?

6. *Can you handle the show's dance requirements?* Some musicals have few dance requirements, some demand a great deal. *South Pacific* doesn't, *Oklahoma!* and *Carousel* do. *My Fair Lady* doesn't, *West Side Story* does.

7. *Can you handle the show's technical requirements?* How many sets are needed? How realistic do they need to be? Do you have room to store sets off stage when not in use? Are there special lighting or

sound requirements? Special effects? If you can't fly your Peter Pan, perhaps you ought to look elsewhere for a show.

8. *Can you easily (and affordably) costume the show?* Period shows such as *Oklahoma!* and *My Fair Lady* demand much more time and money than plays set in contemporary America. And big shows require more resources than small ones.

9. *Can you afford the show?* Royalties can be expensive, as can costumes and sets. Popular musicals typically cost more than straight plays. Figure a rough budget in your head as you consider a particular show. Does it match the average expense for shows you're doing now, or is it a quantum leap into the unknown?

10. *Is the show available?* Surprisingly, not all musicals you might want to produce are available, particularly the newest ones or those being revived at major theaters in New York or other areas of the country. Check with the publisher or royalty house to be sure.

11. *Does the show fit with the rest of your season?* Most successful companies alternate comedy and drama, old and new, musical and nonmusical. That way, they can balance their offerings and build audiences.

12. *Is the show one that will appeal to actors, designers, and production staff?* If it doesn't excite their imagination, it's not likely to get the psychological and hands-on support it needs to succeed.

13. *Do you really want to do the show?* Avoid producing or directing anything that you would not have chosen yourself. There is so much work involved that enthusiasm for a musical is all-important.

"Let's Go on with the Show" 4

Fifty-Six Strong Candidates to Consider

*I*f you're new to musical theater or are just browsing the possibilities, take a look over the alphabetical lists that follow and their descriptions. We've indicated in parentheses the royalty house or publisher that can issue production rights. A list of these sources is given at the end of Chapter 6, "Where Am I Going, and What Will I Find?"

The Classics

ANNIE (STROUSE & CHARNIN)

Audiences seem not to tire of this rags-to-riches tale of a street-smart orphan who out-maneuvers the wily Miss Hannigan in order to become the adopted daughter of the world's richest man. Cartoon humor is balanced with sweetness, and although the second act lacks the energy of the first, the first half's musical numbers ("Tomorrow," "The Hard-Knock Life," "Little Girls," "N.Y.C.") provide enough energy to sustain interest. A great show for a talented group of youngsters as Annie's orphan pals. (Music Theatre International)

ANNIE GET YOUR GUN (BERLIN)

Strong story, great songs ("There's No Business Like Show Business," "They Say It's Wonderful," "Anything You Can Do"), and a large cast. Shooting match at the end raises technical problems (and more, if you're a school), as well as objections to perceived sexism in the 1946 original. Multiple settings and costumes. (Rodgers & Hammerstein Music Library)

ANYTHING GOES (PORTER)

Mostly fast and funny, with emphasis on farce and dance. Songs include "I Get a Kick out of You," "Blow, Gabriel Blow," and the title song. The 1962 off-Broadway script (with songs interpolated from other Porter shows) is the most commonly produced version of this 1934 classic. Sensitivity needed in portrayal of two Asian characters. Mid-sized cast can be small or augmented by chorus and dancers, as needed. Simple set needs. (Tams-Witmark Music Library)

Brigadoon (Lerner & Loewe)

Romantic 1947 fantasy set in Scotland is more dramatic than comic, alternating operetta-style numbers such as "There but for You Go I" and "The Heather on the Hill" with musical comedy relief in "My Mother's Wedding Day" and "Almost Like Being in Love." Large cast, heavy costume demands. Scottish dancers and bagpipers needed for wedding sequence; technical effect of village appearing and disappearing can be handled with scrim and lighting. (Tams-Witmark Music Library)

Bye, Bye, Birdie (Strouse & Adams)

While Elvis's 1957 induction into the military may have been its inspiration, this 1960 musical has transcended that moment of pop history. It's still a popular production, particularly with high schools or community theaters with a large number of teenaged performers. Songs include "Put on a Happy Face," "Rosie," "Talk to Me," and "A Lot of Living to Do." Large cast, multiple sets. (Tams-Witmark Music Library)

Cabaret (Kander & Ebb)

The stage version is quite different from the film, but it's still a dark commentary on 1920s Berlin and its slide into the world of the Third Reich. While the songs are excellent ("Cabaret," "Willkommen," "Don't Tell Mama," "Married," "Tomorrow Belongs to Me"), modern productions tend to cast actors who can sing rather than singers who can act. The overtly sexual nature of much of the show is a challenge for some theater companies, as are the anti-Jewish sentiments expressed by some of the characters. (Tams-Witmark Music Library)

Carousel (Rodgers & Hammerstein)

The darkest of the R&H musicals, this is almost operatic in its exploration of love, relationships, and responsibility. Songs include "What's the Use of Wond'rin'," "If I Loved You," "June Is Busting out All Over," and "You'll Never Walk Alone." Large cast, strong voices needed for the five principals; ballet sequence. (Rodgers & Hammerstein Music Library)

CHICAGO (KANDER & EBB)

A story of murder, desire, and the media, this is a musical without a heart—and intentionally so. Thus, it's important that the performers playing Roxie and Velma have a natural warmth that helps the audience past the characters' inherent selfishness. The show's relentless sexuality and crassness make this one difficult for some companies to pull off. (Co-editor Stephen Peithman saw a production in which teenaged girls were used as dancers; the result was disconcerting—and not in the way the authors intended.) Songs include "Razzle-Dazzle," "All That Jazz," and "Nowadays." This is a heavy dance show, and one of the characters is a male who sings soprano. (Samuel French)

A CHORUS LINE (HAMLISCH & KLEBAN)

This was groundbreaking in 1976 and still holds up well, for the most part. Because it's about dancers auditioning for a Broadway show, don't attempt this unless you have dancers who can also act and sing. Once there, the show provides a remarkable series of vignettes for individual performers, as well as two rousing choruses of the showstopping "One." Other highlights include "Dance 10, Looks 3" and "What I Did for Love." (Tams-Witmark Music Library)

FIDDLER ON THE ROOF (BOCK & HARNICK)

Frequently produced, but often without a sense of the human drama that lies underneath. The show calls for a charismatic leading man who can help audiences understand the seriousness of the characters' situation, as well as the need for humor to help them survive through it all. Songs include "Sunrise, Sunset," "Tradition," and "If I Were a Rich Man." Large cast, simple set requirements. (Music Theatre International)

A FUNNY THING HAPPENED ON THE WAY TO THE FORUM (SONDHEIM)

A burlesque-style rendition of a Roman farce, with a hilarious story line and a delightful score ("Comedy Tonight," "Lovely," "Everybody Ought to Have a Maid"). Needs a strong male lead and a director who can keep things moving. (Music Theatre International)

GODSPELL (SCHWARTZ)

A pop-biblical revue whose vaudeville-style take on the gospel has transcended its 1970s trappings. Songs by Stephen Schwartz include

"Day by Day," "Prepare Ye the Way of the Lord," and "Save the People." Simple sets, costumes, and staging have made this popular with community theaters across the country. (Music Theatre International)

GREASE (JACOBS & CASEY)

Like *Bye, Bye, Birdie* but without its quality or charm, *Grease* nonetheless tapped into 1950s nostalgia with great effectiveness—so who are we to complain? Songs include "Summer Nights," "We Go Together," and "Look at Me, I'm Sandra Dee." (Note: Songs written for the film version, including "You're the One That I Want" and "Hopelessly Devoted to You" are not part of the stage package.) (Samuel French)

GUYS AND DOLLS (LOESSER)

Some call this the best musical comedy ever written, and we won't disagree. Clever plot and delightful characters support a strong score ("I've Never Been in Love Before," "I'll Know," "If I Were a Bell," "Luck Be a Lady"). Multiple sets, large cast, extensive choreography. (Music Theatre International)

GYPSY (STYNE & SONDHEIM)

Like *Fiddler on the Roof*, this 1959 musical depends on a charismatic actor in the lead role (Mama Rose). Large cast includes children in singing/dancing roles, strippers in Act II. Songs include "Everything's Coming Up Roses," "Small World," "Let Me Entertain You," and "Together, Wherever We Go." The burlesque-show scenes and the mother/daughter relationship demand mature actors to bring them off. (Tams-Witmark Music Library)

HELLO, DOLLY! (HERMAN)

Big and brassy, and again dependent on a strong lead actor, this show needs to be kept moving by a strong director/choreographer or team. Songs include "It Only Takes a Moment," "Before the Parade Passes By," and the title song. Large cast with heavy period costume needs; multiple settings. (Tams-Witmark Music Library)

HOW TO SUCCEED IN BUSINESS WITHOUT REALLY TRYING (LOESSER)

A little dated unless played as a period piece, this 1962 Pulitzer Prize winner can still be wonderfully entertaining, as evidenced by its successful 1990s Broadway revival. Songs include "I Believe in You" and

"The Brotherhood of Man." Because the show is heavily satirical, the male lead needs natural warmth to keep the audience on his side. Large cast, many big ensemble numbers. (Music Theatre International)

INTO THE WOODS (SONDHEIM)

One of Sondheim's more popular musicals, this one is a reworking (and interweaving) of familiar fairy tales. Act I gives us the traditional presentation (Grimm's, not Disney's), while Act II tells us what happened after "happily ever after." The strong (and quirky) score includes "No One Is Alone," "Children Will Listen," and the title song. Large cast of individual characters (no chorus), some tricky technical effects. (Music Theatre International)

JESUS CHRIST SUPERSTAR (LLOYD WEBBER & RICE)

Recounting the last seven days of Jesus in contemporary terms, this rock opera is usually performed with microphones, so it needs singers familiar with the technical issues. Songs include "I Don't Know How to Love Him" and the title tune, but all blend rock sound with revivalist fervor. Staging can be simple to extravagant. (Music Theatre International)

JOSEPH AND THE AMAZING TECHNICOLOR DREAMCOAT (LLOYD WEBBER & RICE)

A great favorite with young-people's theater, this eclectic mix of musical styles is a bit disjointed, but offers a large number of singing roles and can be augmented by chorus and dancers as desired. Songs in this retelling of the biblical story of Joseph and his brothers include "Any Dream Will Do" and the Elvis-flavored "Song of the King." (Music Theatre International)

THE KING AND I (RODGERS & HAMMERSTEIN)

A wonderful show with huge demands on costumes, sets, and voices. Songs include "Shall We Dance," "Hello, Young Lovers," "Getting to Know You," and "Something Wonderful." Ballet: "Small House of Uncle Thomas." Sensitivity needed in handling of Asian setting and characters. (Rodgers & Hammerstein Music Library)

KISS ME, KATE (PORTER)

Cole Porter's best score and best show, with a battling, formerly married pair of actors dueling it out during rehearsal and performance of a musical version of *The Taming of the Shrew*. Strong acting and singing demands for the principals, with sophisticated comedy in the dialogue and sexual innuendo in the lyrics. Large cast, heavy costume needs (modern and Elizabethan), and many dance numbers. (Tams-Witmark Music Library)

A LITTLE NIGHT MUSIC (SONDHEIM)

This tribute to operetta and three-quarter time is a sophisticated fairy tale about chances squandered and love regained. This exceptional musical needs exceptional singer/actors in almost every role, for songs like "Send in the Clowns," "You Must Meet My Wife," "Every Day a Little Death," "Remember?," and "A Weekend in the Country." Heavy demand for period costumes, plus frequent scene changes in Act I. (Music Theatre International)

LITTLE SHOP OF HORRORS (MENCKEN & ASHMAN)

An offbeat spoof of the horror genre, it uses an effective pastiche of 1960s Motown styles to tell the story of a man, a woman, and a human-eating plant named Audrey II. The score includes "Somewhere That's Green," "Skid Row," and the title song. Small cast, simple sets; Audrey II needed in several sizes, and must be constructed exactly to specifications or rented. (Music Theatre International)

MAME (HERMAN)

This musical version of *Auntie Mame* rests firmly on the shoulders of its leading lady. Expertly blending comedy and sentiment, the show's songs include "We Need a Little Christmas," "If He Walked into My Life," and "Mame." Large cast; multiple scenes, sets, and costumes. (Tams-Witmark Music Library)

MAN OF LA MANCHA (LEE & DARION)

A difficult show to pull off because of acting, vocal, and technical demands; when done well, this has strong audience appeal. Best-known song in this retelling of the Don Quixote story is "The Impossible Dream." Leading man must be an actor with Shakespearean range and big singing voice; female lead must have strength in both chest and head range. "Rape Ballet" is strong stuff for some, and should be handled with care. Single set, but calls for staircase to be raised and lowered several times. (Tams-Witmark Music Library)

THE MUSIC MAN (WILLSON)

This tale of a charming con man (Harold Hill) needs a strong male lead, but shares the musical wealth with the large cast that includes a strong soprano (Marian) and a roving barbershop quartet. Period costumes and many sets, several large production numbers. Songs include "Seventy-Six Trombones," "'Til There Was You," "Gary, Indiana," and "Trouble." (Music Theatre International)

MY FAIR LADY (LERNER & LOEWE)

A wonderful score ("I Could Have Danced All Night," "Wouldn't It Be Loverly," "On the Street Where You Live," "I've Grown Accustomed to Her Face") and story (derived from Shaw's *Pygmalion*). Note that Eliza is the only female lead; the second female lead (Mrs. Higgins) is a non-singer. Many sets and period costumes. (Tams-Witmark Music Library)

NO, NO, NANETTE (YOUMANS)

This 1925 musical comedy was refurbished for its hit 1971 Broadway revival. The silly plot is really an excuse for comedy, production numbers, and songs like "Tea for Two," "I Want to Be Happy," and "Two Many Rings Around Rosie." Large cast, period costumes, several large sets. (Tams-Witmark Music Library)

OKLAHOMA! (RODGERS & HAMMERSTEIN)

A simple (and occasionally darkly dramatic) story is bolstered by a fine score ("Oh, What a Beautiful Morning," "People Will Say We're in Love," "Out of My Dreams," and the title song). Heavy dance show, including the famous "Dream Ballet" ending Act I. Simple sets. Sensitivity needed in portrayal of the sexually obsessed Jud Fry. (Rodgers & Hammerstein Music Library)

OLIVER! (BART)

Dickens's *Oliver Twist* is given a fine musical treatment, with songs such as "Consider Yourself," "Who Will Buy?," "Where Is Love?," and "As Long as He Needs Me." Like *Carousel*, this is often dark, with thievery, violence, and murder playing important roles in the action. A large number of child performers needed. Multiple sets. (Tams-Witmark Music Library)

ONCE UPON A MATTRESS (RODGERS & BARER)

Carol Burnett made her Broadway debut in this modern version of the fairy tale about the princess and the pea. Silly and cartoonish, and utterly hilarious, the show needs strong comic performers, particularly in the roles of the princess, the prince, and the queen. The charming score includes "Normandy," "Shy," "I'm in Love with a Girl Named Fred," and "In a Little While." Mid-sized cast can be augmented; simple set except for the bed with twenty mattresses. (Rodgers & Hammerstein Music Library)

THE PAJAMA GAME (ADLER & ROSS)

Union strife in a pajama factory is the unlikely setting for this 1954 classic. Songs include "Hey There," "Hernando's Hideaway," "Once-a-Year Day," "There Once Was a Man," and "Steam Heat." The bright and breezy show has a large cast, three major dance numbers, and many set changes—from factory to house by the train tracks, from outdoor picnic to indoor labor rally. (Music Theatre International)

PETER PAN (CHARLAP, LEIGH, STYNE, COMDEN, GREEN)

The familiar story is buoyed by a fine score ("I Gotta Crow," "Never Never Land") and two lead roles to die for. Technical issues are the only concerns here. Peter and the children must fly, and this raises multiple issues relating to the stage area, set design, and safety. The firm, Flying by Foy, can provide the necessary equipment, training, and technical assistance. (Samuel French)

SHOW BOAT (KERN & HAMMERSTEIN)

A landmark musical, this show should be attempted only by companies able to handle the huge, sprawling production demands, as well as having a large cast of African American performers. Songs include "Old Man River," "Can't Help Loving That Man," "Make Believe," and "Bill." Unusually large cast, extensive sets, and costumes. (Rodgers & Hammerstein Music Library)

THE SOUND OF MUSIC (RODGERS & HAMMERSTEIN)

A great favorite with family audiences. Many community theaters choose this because of the large cast, giving many people a chance to be on stage, particularly women and children (their friends and family can fill a theater). The only down side is that many people come expecting the film version, which is different in many respects from the original. The play has two numbers for Elsa and Max ("How Can Love Survive?" and "There's No Way to Stop It") and another for Maria and Captain Von Trapp ("An Ordinary Couple"). Two songs written for the film ("I Have Confidence" and "Something Good") are available upon request. (Rodgers & Hammerstein Music Library)

SOUTH PACIFIC (RODGERS & HAMMERSTEIN)

This musical play deftly balances comedy and drama, with a strong message about racial understanding. Songs include "Some Enchanted Evening," "Younger Than Springtime," "A Wonderful Guy," and "There Is Nothing Like a Dame." Strong voices needed for leads; separate men's and women's choruses provide opportunities for many to shine. Show designed with minimal choreography, few sets, simple costumes. (Rodgers & Hammerstein Music Library)

SWEET CHARITY (COLEMAN & FIELDS)

The whole is greater than the sum of its parts in this tale of an ever-optimistic dancehall hostess and her search for happiness. Designed for a lead (and two friends) who can dance, sing, and act, this is not an easy show to cast. With the right people and a strong choreographer, it can be pure theatrical magic. The score includes "Big Spender," "Where Am I Going?," "Baby, Dream Your Dream," and "If My Friends Could See Me Now." Simple sets and costumes. (Tams-Witmark Music Library)

WEST SIDE STORY (BERNSTEIN & SONDHEIM)

This 1957 story about gang violence rises or falls on its dancing, as well as the strong voices of its Tony, Maria, and Anita. Songs include "Maria," "I Feel Pretty," "Somewhere," and "America." Originally directed by a choreographer (Jerome Robbins), the show needs a firm hand to keep it visually as well as vocally exciting. Simple sets. (Music Theatre International)

YOU'RE A GOOD MAN, CHARLIE BROWN (GESNER)

A charming six-person revue based on the Charles Schulz comic strips, this show works on two levels. Children love the escapades of the familiar "Peanuts" characters; adults enjoy the psychological and satirical insights. The delightful score includes "Happiness" and "Suppertime." Simple set and costumes. (Tams-Witmark Music Library)

Overlooked Gems

110 IN THE SHADE (JONES & SCHMIDT)

An effective and well-crafted musicalization of *The Rainmaker*. A large cast and a fine score. (Tams-Witmark Music Library)

BABES IN ARMS (RODGERS & HART)

Teenaged children of vaudevillians get together to put on a show. Fast-paced and laden with hits ("I Wish I Were in Love Again," "The Lady Is a Tramp," "My Funny Valentine," "Johnny One-Note," "Where or When"). (Rodgers & Hammerstein Music Library)

BELLS ARE RINGING (STYNE, COMDEN, GREEN)

A funny although somewhat sprawling show, this needs a strong comic actress in the lead (it was written for Judy Holliday) and an imaginative set designer. The score includes "Just in Time" and "The Party's Over." (Tams-Witmark Music Library)

THE BOYS FROM SYRACUSE (RODGERS & HART)

Shakespeare's *The Comedy of Errors* set to extraordinary music ("Falling in Love with Love," "Sing for Your Supper," and "This Can't Be Love"). A large cast, including four men who can pass as two sets of twins. (Rodgers & Hammerstein Music Library)

CARNIVAL (MERRILL)

An orphan girl is swept up in the color and romance of a traveling European carnival, including a complicated relationship with a difficult puppeteer and his creations. A strong soprano is needed for the central role of Lili, and a good choreographer to keep things moving. The score includes "Love Makes the World Go 'Round." (Tams-Witmark Music Library)

DAMES AT SEA (WISE, HAIMSOHN, MILLER)

Six hardworking singer/dancers re-create the Busby Berkeley 1930s musical with a delightful original score, including "It's You," "That Mister Man of Mine," and "Raining in My Heart." Simple sets, but several costume quick-changes. (Samuel French)

DAMN YANKEES (ADLER & ROSS)

A middle-aged baseball fan sells his soul to the devil to become a young baseball player who can lead his team to victory. Large cast (mostly male) needs charismatic devil and his female assistant. Score includes "Whatever Lola Wants" and "Heart." (Music Theatre International)

THE FANTASTICKS (JONES & SCHMIDT)

The longest running musical in history (it opened off-off-Broadway in 1960 and is still going), this small-cast show blends romance, adventure, and a certain edge. The score includes "Try to Remember" and "Soon It's Gonna Rain." (Music Theatre International)

FIORELLO! (BOCK & HARNICK)

The true story of New York Mayor Fiorello La Guardia won a Pulitzer Prize. Fine character studies and a score that includes "'Til Tomorrow" and "Politics and Poker." (Tams-Witmark Music Library)

L'IL ABNER (DEPAUL & MERCER)

The comic strip is long gone, but the musical continues to entertain. Silly and endearing, the show needs a strong choreographer and dancers. The score includes "Jubilation T. Cornpone," "Namely You," and "The Country's in the Very Best of Hands." (Tams-Witmark Music Library)

LITTLE MARY SUNSHINE (BESOYAN)

A spoof of *Rose-Marie* and related operettas, this off-Broadway hit is still a charmer, although some object to the "Me Injun Chief" dialogue (even though it also is a spoof). Mid-sized cast; original used two-piano accompaniment. (Samuel French)

LITTLE JOHNNY JONES (COHAN)

Heavily rewritten for modern audiences, this old-time classic still has much to recommend it. The tale of an American jockey accused of throwing the English Derby, it includes songs such as "I'm a Yankee Doodle Dandy" and "Give My Regards to Broadway." (Tams-Witmark Music Library)

Man with a Load of Mischief [Clifton & Tarver]

A real find—a six-character musical drama set in an English wayside inn. Strong voices for the two leads, but all six characters get to sing some fine songs, including "Come to the Masquerade," "Romance!," and the title tune. (Samuel French)

Romance/Romance (Herrmann & Harmon)

Two one-act musicals, one set in the nineteenth century, the other in the 1980s, with four actors playing all the roles. The first act is more comic, the second more serious. A fine score and an intriguing concept. (Samuel French)

She Loves Me (Bock & Harnick)

Two workers in a European parfumerie dislike each other, not realizing they are corresponding under pen names through a lonely-hearts club—and falling in love. A charming show in all respects. The score includes "Will He Like Me?" and the title song. (Tams-Witmark Music Library)

Wonderful Town (Bernstein, Comden, Green)

My Sister Eileen set to music (including "Ohio," "A Little Bit in Love," "It's Love"), with a large cast dominated by the character of Ruth (written for Rosalind Russell). If you have a lot of good people to show off, this one might do it. (Tams-Witmark Music Library)

"It's Today" | 5

With so many choices to select from, what basis should you use to choose? One possible method to consider is trying to capitalize on what's happening around you.

Finding Contemporary Tie-ins to Older Musicals

Lisa Viall

I t's strange that during the height of the *Titanic* craziness in the late 1990s—both the film and the Broadway musical—not many theaters chose to produce *The Unsinkable Molly Brown*, the original *Titanic*-inspired vehicle from the 1960s. Yes, it is a tough show to cast and not an extremely well-known title, but think about the potential audience that could have been attracted to it because of the tie-in.

Similarly, the impeachment hearings that dominated the news for months could have been perfectly played out on stage with a production of *Of Thee I Sing*, the Gershwin classic. Though written in the early 1930s, the show deals with the rise and (almost) fall of the President of the United States, casting a satirical eye on the office of the Vice President and the man who holds it.

The main aspect of picking a show that is germane to a current event or a community is research. This does not have to be as daunting as it seems. What events have happened around the globe, in the country, in your community, or in your school that could somehow be paralleled on stage? You don't even have to say, "We're doing this because it relates to that." Let the audience figure it out.

Was there a recent labor dispute, contract negotiation, or strike anywhere in your area? In the lighthearted musical classic, *The Pajama Game*, the main conflict is about a seven-and-a-half-cent raise. There even is a union rally, where the show-stopping number "Steam Heat" is performed.

How did the Little Leaguers do this year? Is there a new ball park being built nearby? Do you live in or near a town that has a major- or minor-league team? If so, the time-honored crowd pleaser, *Damn Yankees*, may be the show for you. Is there a Catholic school in your community? Are they looking to produce a show? If so, there is always *Do Black Patent Leather Shoes Really Reflect Up?* or *Nunsense.*

A show could be devoted to serious issues as well. Suppose a particular slot in your season falls close to AIDS Awareness Week. Two shows that tap into this subject are *Falsettos* and *The Last Session.* Because of the theme, these are sometimes presented as a fund-raising event, sponsored in association with an AIDS or gay-rights organization. This is a very effective way to introduce new people to your theater.

Scheduling shows around seasonal observances such as Christmas, Hannukah, Halloween, or Independence Day is common. However, there are many more with immediate social or historical relevance, including Black History Month (February), Women's History Month (March), and Family History Month (October).

Read licensing-group catalogues for plot synopses to see how they can relate to a current news event or trend. But also bear in mind that sometimes a show and an event just don't fit together, and it would not be in your company's best interest to force issues that aren't there or that seem to capitalize unfeelingly on recent events. But when the combination meshes well, both the theater and the audience will reap enormous benefits from the production.

"Where Am I Going, and What Will I Find?" 6

Locating and Using Sources for Musicals

*H*ow do you find the right musical when you have mostly female or male actors? No one to build elaborate sets? A cast all over the age of fifty? A minuscule budget—or stage?

The answer may lie in the most obvious place—catalogues of plays, in print or online. This is the best way to identify titles that meet your requirements, particularly online catalogues with searchable databases.

Not all publishers feature musicals, and a few offer only musicals. We've listed the principal ones in this chapter. You will find a complete list of play publishers on the website of the American Association of Community Theatre at <www. aact.org>.

How to Use Play Catalogues

"This year we purchased forty-eight scripts at $6 each," a reader wrote us. "We hope to select four to stage. To date, we have rejected twenty-seven and accepted two. When you consider the cost and time, we have wasted a great deal over the years. The play catalogues offer only brief descriptions and many are a bit misleading. How can you know what's really good? They do not have a rating system that would let us know about offensive or just plain boring content. One script sounded great but turned out to be very offensive and a bit boring. On the other hand, we almost missed another that turned out to be wonderful. But how do we know when looking in the catalogues? How can we learn to read catalogues better?"

Good question. However, it's important not to expect more from catalogues than they were intended to deliver.

They are, after all, sales pieces, not impartial commentary. And even if play catalogues did provide critical commentary, whose judgment would it reflect? How would it correlate with your taste, your audience, your community, and your strengths (or weaknesses) as a theater company?

The truth is, only you know what will work best for your theater and your audience. No one else can determine that for you.

What a play catalogue *can* do is tell you that a musical is available, as well as give you a plot outline, cast breakdown, songs, orchestration, and something about length and set requirements. It's unrealistic to ask for more.

To cut down the time spent on reading unsuitable plays, you need to do your homework first. There are two different ways to do this.

The first approach is to look through the catalogues and create a list of the musicals that may be worth reading. Then find out if they have been reviewed in national magazines or major metropolitan newspapers. Publications to check include *Stage Directions*, *American Theatre*, *Dramatics*, and such general-interest magazines as *Time* and *Newsweek*, *The New Yorker*, and of course, *The New York Times*. Other resources are *The Best Plays* annuals and the bound volumes of the New York drama critics reviews. Online, you can visit *Curtain Up* at <www.curtainup.com>. You also can search the worldwide web to find out what other companies are producing. You'll find a list of community-theater companies, for example, on the website of the American Association of Community Theatre at <www.aact.org>.

A second approach is to keep an ongoing card (or computer) file of plays as you read about them in these same publications. Then, when you see these same plays appear in the catalogues, you can consult your file. The advantage is that the file will contain only those plays and musicals that you know are of interest to you.

What about musicals that have not been produced or for which you cannot find reviews? One answer is to find out as much as you can about the playwright and composer. If he or she has a strong reputation for other plays, chances are good that this one will be at least worth consideration.

Finally, encourage company members to read widely and stay informed about new plays and theater in general. Go to as many plays as you can. Seeing one musical by an unknown composer can tell you something about other works by the same person. Keep up with the productions that other groups in your region are doing and share information with them. Join your regional theater alliance—or help start one.

Play selection is not an exact science, but armed with more information, you can reduce frustration and increase your chances for success.

Sources

The following four publishers are the chief source for most Broadway and off-Broadway musicals. All have catalogues for the asking, as well as websites.

■ Music Theatre International; 421 W. 54th St., New York, NY 10019; 212/541-4684; <www.mtishows.com>

■ Rodgers & Hammerstein Theatre Library; 229 W. 28th St., 11th floor, New York, NY 10001; 212/564-4000; <www.rnh.com/theatre/index.html>

■ Samuel French; 45 W. 25th St., New York, NY 10010; 212/206-8990; <www.samuelfrench.com>

■ Tams-Witmark Music Library; 560 Lexington Ave., New York, NY 10022; 800/221-7196; <www.tams-witmark.com>

While these are the principal sources for musicals, scripts and scores for musical productions are also available from other publishers, including the following:

■ Eldridge Publishing Co.; P.O. Box 1595, Venice, FL 34284; 800/HI-STAGE; <www.histage.com>.

■ Encore Performance Publishing; 92 N. 970 W., Orem, UT 84057; 801/225-0605; <www.encoreplay.com>

■ I. E. Clark Publications; P.O. Box 246, Schulenburg, TX 78956-0246; 409/743-3232

■ Pioneer Drama Service; P.O. Box 426, Englewood, CO 80155; 800/333-7262; <www.pioneerdrama.com>

7 | "I'd Rather Be Right"

Playing by the Rules

U nless you are planning on writing your own, if you want to produce a musical, you must obtain the rights to the work. All theater companies must deal with performance rights and royalties (and not just for musicals, of course). However, while it may be a common concern, it is also not universally understood, nor are copyright rules always strictly honored. And the question of rights for a musical is additionally complicated.

Here are answers to the most frequently asked questions about this subject.

Why Copyright and Royalties?

A musical play is the artistic creation of the composer, lyricist, and librettist. Fairness—and the law—dictate that the creators deserve recompense for their labors. Copyright law protects authors' basic rights over their work: the rights to perform or display it publicly, to reproduce and distribute it and produce other works based on it, to claim its authorship, and to make sure its integrity is not compromised. A work is copyrighted by the act of writing something and is announced publicly by the act of publishing the text. A copyrighted play then can become a rentable property.

Think of it this way: an apartment owner can establish certain conditions or restrictions under which a property may be rented. You, as a prospective tenant, can choose to accept or refuse those terms. If you refuse, you look somewhere else. If you accept the terms, you must follow the owner's written rules, as long as they are legal. And you can't live in the apartment without paying the rent—at least, not for long.

It seems odd that while the concept of renting an apartment is easily understood, the concept of renting a play seems difficult for many people. Publisher I.E. Clark states the concept simply enough: "Royalty is the author's income, the rental he receives for the use of his property. Like other legitimate play publishers, we pay our authors a royalty on each book sold and a substantial percentage of the performance royalty we collect."

In the case of plays, the copyright information is clearly stated in the printed text, usually on the opposite side of the title page. More detailed information is included in the licensing contract, but the basics are printed on the copyright page.

A license to present a show typically contains general rules, as well as specifics such as the dates for which performance rights are granted, the theater location, the number of seats, and the price of tickets. Note that the license is specific in its wording and does not imply any authorization to move the production to another theater, to extend the run, to change prices, or to modify the play in any way.

Which Musicals Are Under Copyright?

As a rule of thumb, it's safe to assume that something's fallen out of copyright if it was first published more than seventy-five years ago. This covers the twenty-eight-year term of the original copyright plus an additional forty-seven years for possible copyright renewal. Note that, occasionally, plays existed in manuscript for some time before being published, and because copyright protection begins with publication date, they may still be protected.

For theater companies, the main problem lies in recent translations or new "performing editions" of older musicals. The original may be in the public domain, but if the new performing edition is fewer than seventy-five years old, it is probably protected by copyright law.

What is most frustrating is that there is no one place you can go to find out the copyright status of any given work or version. Instead, start with play catalogues. Then, if you have no luck, you can contact the Library of Congress, which will search for a small fee; however, because of the sheer volume of acquisitions and the constraints of budget cuts, the response may be slow. (Write Information Section, U.S. Copyright Office; Library of Congress; Washington, D.C. 20559; 202/707-3000. The office has a variety of booklets available for the asking, which also can be found online at <www.loc.gov>.)

What Does the Publisher/Agent Do?

Previously, we likened production rights to renting an apartment. Although you might go directly to the owner of the apartment building, you might be more likely to contact a rental agent who handles the transaction on behalf of the owner.

Likewise, the creators of a musical normally authorize an agent to handle the business of assigning production rights. The agent may be an individual, but most often is a publisher or "royalty house," such as Samuel French or Music Theatre International. In essence, the publisher acts as the author's agent, collecting a small percentage (10 to 20 percent) for handling the licensing agreements.

The arrangement is a delicate one. The publisher must follow the requirements set by the playwright and the copyright law. At the same time, the publisher is in a business that demands satisfying customer needs.

"Our own philosophy," says I.E. Clark, "and one shared by most of the major publishers, is that the publisher/agent is the liaison between the author and the producing organization. We try to give our customers the best terms and the best service we can as limited by our contracts with our playwrights. We also try our best to see that our authors realize enough income from their work to encourage them to continue writing. Nothing pleases us more than to send a playwright a big fat royalty check made up of payments from happy producers."

Why Is There Royalty on Free Performances?

Royalty covers the performance of a play for an audience, regardless of the circumstances. "Whenever there is an audience, we charge a royalty," says Craig Pospisil of Dramatic Publishing Co. "If the work is done strictly in a classroom for a class, then it doesn't really constitute a performance. But if the class invites in an audience of parents or even another class, then it's a performance and subject to royalties."

Another example is the custom of inviting friends, family, and other guests to a final dress rehearsal "to get the feel of a live audience." The operative word here is *audience*. This is a performance and would trigger the royalty clause. However, because the performance is free and given to a small number of people, the royalty charged likely will be small.

It's up to the play-leasing company, not the producer, to decide whether a particular presentation is an actual performance. If you're in doubt, contact the publisher/agent. But more to the point, says Clark, "We ask, 'Why don't you charge admission?' We realize that there are performances at school assemblies, workshops, club meetings, and so on, where it would be impossible or unwise to charge admission. But we are appalled when a principal tells a teacher that admission may not be charged for a public performance. When was the last time the school had an admission-free football or basketball game? Why should drama be a second-class citizen to athletics?"

Why Are There No Discounts for Nonprofit Groups?

The royalty fees listed in the publisher's catalogue are the rates established for nonprofessional theaters. Professional theaters apply for a leasing fee and are charged differently.

Can Fees Be Reduced?

Yes and no. However, most publishers prefer not to talk specifically about such reductions. Says Clark, "That depends on many things, most of which we do not want to discuss publicly. It is a private matter between us and our customers. We are willing to consider such requests, but most of the time we say no."

Aileen Hussung of Samuel French mentions two situations that might allow a reduction. "Since royalties are in part determined by the number of seats you can sell, you can block off auditorium seats and ask for a lower royalty than would normally be the case. If you're a good customer, and the show doesn't do well, you may be able to get a reduction of royalty after the fact."

When Is the Royalty Due?

Check your licensing agreement. In almost all cases, you must pay several weeks prior to the first performance.

How Is Copyright Violated—
and How Is That Violation Discovered?

The most frequent violation is presenting a play without permission and without paying royalty.

"Of course, some violations are unintentional," says Clark. "We occasionally receive a letter from a high school director telling us that he or she ordered one copy of a certain play and is enclosing the royalty payment. When we ask where he got copies for the whole cast, he replied that he photocopied them; he had no idea that he was breaking the law.

"We have found very few violations by colleges and universities and by church schools," Clark continues. "High schools are generally honest. Perhaps the most frequent type of cheating by high schools and junior highs is paying royalty for one or two performances and then presenting three or four."

With so many theaters scattered all over the country, one might think that most cheaters can get away with royalty violations. Obviously, many do. But a surprising number don't, and for reasons they might never suspect.

Most publishers subscribe to clipping services that regularly monitor newspapers for ads and articles about theater productions. These are then checked against the company's list of licensees. A surprising number of violations turn up in other ways, however, says Clark.

"An acquaintance who has moved to another state writes me, 'I saw a great performance of Play X by ABC High School last night.' Or a director: 'I saw a performance of Play Y and I'd like to order a copy.' Or customers: 'The Z Theater did the same play we did, and I thought you'd like to know that our performance was better.'"

Rival theater companies have been known to turn in offenders as well. The Rodgers & Hammerstein Theatre Library reports it gets up to a dozen anonymous tips a week. Violations turn up in quite unexpected ways. A playwright sent a publisher a manuscript and, as proof that his play had been performed, he also sent the printed program that just happened to list other plays performed by the same theater company—including one from that publisher that had been produced without permission.

"Under all these circumstances, we check our files to see that books had been ordered and royalty paid," Clark says. "When we find a violation, we get to work on it."

One of the most blatant violations came to light when an announcement appeared in a Houston newspaper that one of Clark's plays was being performed "by a prestigious local theater. The producer had checked out a copy of the play from the public library, made copies, and presented the play. Another example was a community-theater company in New England that ordered copies of a play and paid the leasing fee for ten performances. We saw a photo from the production in a theater trade publication: the caption under the photo mentioned that the play was performed twelve times." Says Clark, "Our advice to cheaters is: Don't advertise your play, don't tell anybody about it, don't let anybody come to see it."

Can We Make Changes and Cuts?

Most playwrights oppose changes in the text and protection against this is stated in the contract. Cuts or changes in dialogue may seem minor to the director, but can easily alter the author's intentions. In most cases, the license states clearly that the play must be performed as written.

This does not mean that changes are impossible, merely that you must check with the publisher/agent to clear them before you put them into effect. Indeed, most publisher/agents urge directors to contact them regarding possible changes, because there may be an accommodation. The key to acceptance is how the change affects the integrity of the script. Playwrights and their agents are reasonable people, and if your request makes sense, it may be granted.

However, note that most requests are handled on an individual basis. In many cases, the playwright or the playwright's estate must be contacted for permission.

One recent addition to licenses is a "gender clause," which restricts changing a character's sex from female to male or vice versa. This grew out of a lawsuit won by Tams-Witmark Music Library in which a company changed the gender of Reno Sweeney in *Anything Goes* from female to male. Considering that Reno has a romance with a British gentleman in the show, the sex change put an entirely new slant on the plot.

Because changes are not a black-and-white situation, it's a good idea to be certain about them before you present the play. "Always ask," Hussung says. "It never hurts to ask." Make your requests as specific as possible, says Pospisil. "Don't write and ask to 'cut a little bit' out of Act I. Be specific about the cuts, including the specific words and lines and pages."

As you might expect by this point, there is no across-the-board formula regarding excerpting or cutting plays for competition or similar uses. "You can't cut or excerpt Albee, Beckett, or Williams," says Pospisil. "Others may allow it, but each request has to be checked with the author or his or her estate." All the representatives we talked with agreed that it is easier to get approval to do just one act rather than cut down an entire play to fit a time constraint.

Can We Substitute a Song from the Movie Version?

"Composers get livid when you put in songs from the movie version," says Music Theatre International's Steve Spiegel. "And rightly so, since you are altering their work." In most cases, you are not allowed to substitute or add songs in a musical. For example, because many people are most familiar with the film version of *Grease*, many directors are tempted to add songs written for the movie; this violates the license. (The 1990s national touring and Broadway version, however, did negotiate rights to the movie songs.)

When a university theater company asked to add the song "If You Go Away" ("Ne Me Quitte Pas") to the score of *Jacques Brel Is Alive and Well and Living in Paris*, they were denied.

Such substitutions aren't always caught. One reader told us that when the conductor's rental score of *Funny Girl* arrived from the royalty house, he discovered that a previous user had drawn a line through the first page of the overture (which begins with "Don't Rain on My Parade") and written "substitute 'My Man'"—a song used in the film, but not by *Funny Girl*'s composer and lyricist.

How Far in Advance Can We Advertise That We're Doing the Show?

"Always check with the licensing company before you put a show in your season brochure," says Spiegel. "One reason is that touring companies often negotiate city and territorial restrictions. These can happen unexpectedly." Your check is the binder to guarantee that you have rights to the show in most cases. However, contracts allow a royalty house to pull rights—although they seldom do it—and some, like Music Theatre International and Samuel French, say they never do.

Final Thoughts

Royalties, rights, and licensing are integral elements in the process of presenting plays to the public. It's true that the rules are not always clear, mostly because each playwright works out the rules separately and often separately for each play. It's also true that most publisher/ agents want to make it as easy as possible for you to license their productions. After all, they make their money by doing so.

Community theater is the backbone of the business, say both Music Theatre International's Spiegel and Samuel French's Hussung. This means that you do have some leverage, so work with the publisher from the get-go. If you have questions, ask. If you are considering changes, ask. If you have a problem, explain. After all, we're all in this together.

"Some Enchanted Evening" | 8

When you want to put on a musical, the easiest thing to do, of course, is contact any of the royalty houses or publisher/agents and obtain the rights to something that is already tried and true. Take your choice of the classics and the overlooked gems.

But what if you wanted to do something completely different? What if you wanted to take material that's already there and use it to make something new?

Here's some advice on how to do that.

Creating a Musical Revue

When the Abbey Players of Lacey, Washington, were putting together their season a few years ago, they discovered that their November date in the small black-box theater at the Washington Center was up against some stiff competition.

"It would be playing opposite a major production of *Peter Pan* on the main stage," explains director Dennis McDonald. "Wishing to hold our dates on a very busy calendar, we decided to present a production that would be cost-effective and fun."

The choice was a musical revue that had been an idea of McDonald's for a number of years. It would be simple and inexpensive, he assured his company, as well as easy to promote, with a wide appeal. If there were any doubts, they were erased when *The Magic of Broadway* opened and was immediately sold out for the run of the show. Three additional performances were added and they sold out in hours. Hundreds were turned away, McDonald says.

The Magic of Broadway, Too was presented the next year, with additional performances, and also sold out its run.

Benefits

McDonald cites five major benefits to a revue with dialogue.

First, a small fee to Broadcast Music, Inc. (BMI) and/or the American Society of Composers, Authors, and Publishers (ASCAP) music-licensing agencies covers royalties, he explains (more information on this later). Second, "the script is fun and exciting to write. There is so much material available that the writing job becomes a task of reducing the information to only just enough to inform while holding the entertainment level high." Third, the narrative maintains the interest of the audience. Fourth, "You can use a cast of six to twelve, male and female, and really showcase their talent." Fifth, "Your orchestra can and should be simple. We used a baby grand, guitar, and percussion for the first production, and two clavinovas for the second. Both combinations worked," he says.

"Our *Magic* productions are fun, popular, and artistically challenging. I think any group can be successful with this concept."

Structuring the Show

Magic is not an ordinary revue or a concert. It is an historical compilation of the careers of Broadway's greatest composers and their contributions to the development of the Broadway musical. The lives and music of Jerome Kern and Richard Rodgers (the latter's early works, through *Oklahoma!*) were featured in the first edition. George Gershwin and Cole Porter were the composers highlighted in the second production, while the third was devoted entirely to Irving Berlin.

McDonald planned to base his first show on the lives of all five of these composers. However, once he began researching—"going to used bookstores for biographies, old sheet music, anything I could find"—he uncovered so much information that he decided to build the show around Kern and Rodgers alone—Kern in Act I and Rodgers in Act II.

"I didn't want to do a musical revue as much as take the audience on an historical journey through the life of the composers, using their music along the way," he explains. Songs were used in chronological order, with brief snippets of historical narration about the composer's life tying them together.

"Each show has approximately six narratives from one to four minutes long," McDonald says. "For example, in our first show, we opened with operetta music from the early twentieth century, then a narrative on Kern's life, followed by the first series of songs. Then more narrative highlights of Kern's life, then the second series of songs, finishing with *Show Boat*, and finally a narrative of Kern's years in Hollywood, and ending with his death. That ended Act I."

If you think that historical narrative would be boring, consider that most musical-theater composers have led interesting lives. Jerome Kern escaped death when he was delayed in sailing for Europe on the *Lusitania*, which was torpedoed by a German submarine. He was brought back to life after dying on the operating table, and had ten more years of life. Kern turned down *Oklahoma!* and was ready to do *Annie, Get Your Gun* when he collapsed on a New York street with a fatal stroke. He was replaced by Irving Berlin—who was thought to be a has-been at the time—and Berlin went on to write his best score.

Likewise, Cole Porter's career was thought to be over after his legs were crushed in a horse-riding accident, but he went on to write *Kiss Me, Kate*. Lorenz Hart was an unhappy man who drank himself to death—all the while writing some of the wittiest lyrics ever heard on Broadway.

McDonald insists that all musical numbers be set in the original context of the shows from which they came, and as close as possible to the way they were originally performed. This reflects the historical atmosphere provided by the narratives. Songs are chosen through a subjective process. McDonald first researches the composer's life and work, then picks the songs he would like to do. From this list, he chooses those songs he feels have to be done, followed by a list of runners-up until he has about forty-five songs. "There is definitely no lack of music," he says. "Deciding what not to use is the problem." From his list of songs, McDonald shapes the show, which runs two and a half hours, including a fifteen- to twenty-minute intermission. Nothing is set in concrete; songs may be added or dropped throughout the rehearsal process.

Casting and Rehearsing

McDonald stresses the importance of a close working relationship with cast and crew.

"Because this is something we create ourselves, there must be complete cooperation between the director, music director, choreographer, and performers. We encourage input from everyone."

At the same time, he points out, the final decision must reside with the director. "You need to make it clear that, ultimately, one person is in charge," he emphasizes. Cast the strongest voices you have, he says, adding that the ideal cast is eight to ten people—eight singers and two pianists.

"You need a strong romantic tenor and strong soprano. After auditions, hold a sing-through so performers become familiar with the music. Remember, performers in their twenties may have never heard this music before."

The first two weeks of rehearsals is strictly vocal, to be sure that the music can be performed as written. "We don't allow key or lyric changes," McDonald says. The second two weeks, McDonald rehearses only movement and choreography. Each performer has perhaps one duet, three or four solos, and also serves as the backup ensemble to others.

During the first four weeks of rehearsal, performers work only two nights a week. After this, there are three more weeks to run the show and, more important, to cut and move numbers until he has shaped the finished product. McDonald never lets the momentum of rehearsal overshadow his vision of the show. Last year, the big production number, Gershwin's "Love Is Sweeping the Country," was cut the night before dress rehearsal. "I loved the song and wanted to do it, but didn't like the way it looked," he explains.

By the same token, don't be afraid to release a performer from a song or from the cast, he advises. One person quit two weeks before opening. McDonald was talked into letting him back in the show, but after the first weekend of performance, the person was removed. The others in the cast were ready to take his songs and the show was better without him, McDonald says.

Production Values

The Magic of Broadway is performed in a 50 × 50-foot box that seats 125 people. Because the setting is minimal, McDonald concentrates on lighting, using it to bridge song numbers and direct the audience's attention, as well as to provide variety of color and shadow.

The cast likes working in the small theater. It's easier to project the lyrics of the songs and involve the entire audience—and McDonald does emphasize audience participation. Some of the show is performed in the audience area, and there is singing and dancing to and with audience members. In some cases, a song is performed and the audience is then invited to sing along. Much of the revue's success is based on the nostalgia factor.

"This is powerful music," he says. "People of a certain age have grown up with this music. It means a lot to them. It conjures up happy memories. And a lot of them want to share it with their families."

The production does not focus entirely on well-known songs, however. "We did Porter's 'Tale of the Oyster,' which brought the house down," McDonald recalls.

It's a Hit!

The first year, the group scheduled eight performances. "I went to the box office and was told, 'We're sold out and we have a lot of people still wanting seats,'" McDonald recalls. "I told them to sell seats for tomorrow's performance. 'You don't understand,' they told me. 'We're sold out for the entire run!' So we added thirteen more performances and they were also sold out."

It's clear that the Abbey Players have tapped into something that other theater companies will want to consider.

9 | *"Reviewing the Situation"*

S o putting together a musical revue sounds like a pretty good idea? There's just one more thing you need to remember before pushing ahead.

Making Sure Your Revue Is Legal

Putting together a revue based on numbers from Broadway shows has its challenges. One, as mentioned previously, is that performing songs under copyright requires you to get clearance from the publishers. The best way is go through ASCAP or BMI, which represent composers and lyricists. Such clearance, however, has certain limitations. One danger area in particular is the revue that presents a fully staged, costumed production of individual numbers. This, points out Gregory Smith, managing director of Music Theatre International, is a violation of the copyright of the authors.

"The only legal performance of such numbers is without costumes and sets specifying the show's content, with no dialogue used into or around the song, and a valid ASCAP or BMI 'small rights' performance license," Smith says. "Such a performance license does not cover dramatic presentation of such songs, only their performance a la cabaret, or in concert, and normally only three songs from any one musical can be performed."

It's important to remember that members of ASCAP and BMI do not grant these organizations the right to license dramatic performances of their works. While the line between dramatic and nondramatic is not always clear, ASCAP defines a dramatic performance as one that involves using the work to tell a story or as part of a story or plot. Dramatic performances, among others, says ASCAP, include the following:

■ *Performance of an entire "dramatico-musical work."* For example, a performance of the musical play *Oklahoma!* would be a dramatic performance.

■ *Performance of one or more musical compositions from a dramatico-musical work accompanied by dialogue, pantomime, dance, stage action, or visual representation of the work from which the music is taken.* For example, a performance of "People Will Say We're in Love" from *Oklahoma!* with costumes, sets, props, or dialogue from the show would be a dramatic performance.

■ *Performance of one or more musical compositions as part of a story or plot,* whether accompanied or unaccompanied by dialogue, pantomime, dance, stage action, or visual representation. For example, incorporating a performance of "People Will Say We're in Love" into an original or existing play would be considered a dramatic performance of the song.

■ *Performance of a concert version of a dramatico-musical work.* For example, a performance of all the songs in *Oklahoma!,* even without costumes or sets, would be a dramatic performance.

ASCAP and BMI do have the right to license "nondramatic" public performances of its members' works; for example, recordings broadcast on radio, songs or background music performed as part of a movie or other television program, live or recorded performances in a bar or restaurant, or a musical revue that does not involve any of the aspects of "dramatic performance" specifically mentioned.

Because dramatic (or "grand rights") are licensed by the composer or the publisher of the work, Music Theatre International's Smith urges readers to pay particular attention to proper licensing when putting together any original revue.

"Checking with the licensing agency who represents the musical from which the number or numbers come can save a lot of grief during or after production," he says. "It is also wise to check with the music publisher, since some songs need special clearance even for cabaret or concert presentation. 'Adelaide's Lament' from *Guys and*

Dolls is a good case in point—composer Frank Loesser never wanted it performed outside the confines of the show, and his music publisher clears each specific performance.

"Performance rights are a complicated business and asking permission never hurts," Smith adds. "After all, there are plenty of revues already cleared and waiting to be licensed by Music Theatre International and other licensing agencies." Perhaps so, but the urge to create an original revue is very strong in community theater.

To find out which of the two major organizations licenses the music you plan to use, check the sheet music (usually at the bottom of the first page) or recording (usually listed after the song title). ASCAP can be reached at ASCAP Building; One Lincoln Plaza; New York, NY 10023; 212/595-3050. BMI may be reached at 320 West 57th St., New York, NY 10019; 212/586-2000.

Both ASCAP and BMI have helpful websites where you can do a quick search for the works of various composers and lyricists, and also apply for rights online. We find this a major step forward in securing rights. After sending in the online application, we had a quote within a week. The two sites are <www.ascap.com> and <www.bmi.com>.

"I Could Write a Book" | *10*

If your own musical revue was a pleasurable endeavor and the show was a hit for your theater, maybe the time has come to move on to the next step. That next step—your own musical—can seem daunting, which is why it helps to have specific rules to follow.

Ten Steps for Creating Your Own Musical

DIANE SEYMOUR

A playwright, who has had two of his plays produced at a festival where I have served as the dramaturg, recently hired me to critique a script he had written as a book for a musical. In formulating the ideas I wanted to share with him, I came up with ten basics for all writers who are thinking about tackling the musical form.

1. *Collaborate from the start.* It is counterproductive for the playwright to sit down alone and fashion the entire libretto to a musical play first. More than any other writing form, musicals are a collaborative effort. Before a line is written, it's important that the playwright (in musical-theater terms, the *book writer* or *librettist*) and the composer and lyricist meet and discuss the project to make sure all have the same concept and the same goal in mind. You might even want to involve your co-creators in the choice of material to musicalize in the first place, since they most likely will have valuable input on whether the particular material "sings" and is an inherently musical idea.

If you present your collaborators with a play complete with structured scenes, elaborate dialogue, and built-in jokes, you are asking them to fit their music and lyrics into an already tightly knit scheme. They may very well feel hemmed in from the start and may not be able to do their best creative work. Unless you are a gifted musician, lyricist, *and* playwright yourself, writing a musical is a team effort.

2. *Secure rights to the source.* If you are writing a musical play from an original idea, this will not apply. However, since the majority of musicals are based on already-existing stories—that is, films, novels, plays, short stories, and so on—it is crucial that you research the rights before you start to create! Horror stories abound about creative teams spending months or even years writing the "can't-miss" musical version of some famous or even obscure film or play, only to find all their work wasted because the rights to the original underlying material were not available. Unless the material is in the public domain and the copyright has expired, the original author of the work is entitled to a percentage of any work based on it. (These are called *underlying rights.*) If a film or novel has inspired you, you must contact the production company or publisher to find out if the rights are available and how much you must pay up front for the option to use that material. Once you have handled those details, the project can proceed.

3. *Evolve a structure.* Musicals that flow effortlessly seem to be structured around the ideas for musical moments. When you begin to build your show's framework, identify the significant plot moments and build the scenes to those moments, the ones that emotionally cry out to be sung. Then connect the dots as seamlessly as you can to the next significant moment. Once you have outlined them, you can step back and see which ones will be the solo ballads, the duets, the ensemble numbers, or the comedy songs.

Try to get a sense of the piece as a whole. Feel what happens rhythmically from scene to scene: does it need a lift (an up-tempo number), or can the action afford to slow down for a ballad or reflective number (usually after a highly charged, big chorus number, when the audience yearns to rest)? Is comic relief needed at this point? It is often helpful to think of the entire script as a piece of music—similar to the orchestral score of a symphony—to gain that broader perspective.

Also, make sure you bring the music in as soon as possible. That may seem obvious, but I recently saw a libretto where the music didn't begin until page seven—not a very good idea for a show calling itself a musical. (True, the first song in *My Fair Lady* starts about this late, but this new libretto bore no comparison.)

4. *Know your characters.* As in any form of playwriting, it is important to understand the emotional through-lines of your characters—what their needs are and what drives them—before you begin to write. This will help you flesh them out and discover what they would sing about, how they would say it in their own unique way, and what their rhythms and "colors" are. Decide who your protagonist character is; make sure he or she drives the action and is given enough musical numbers to do

that. This kind of detailed information is absolutely essential to your composer and lyricist and helps inform the entire score.

5. *Choose a style.* Once you know your characters, a style for the piece begins to evolve naturally. By style, I mean the way in which different material is treated. Some of the styles you may consider include an old-fashioned book musical, with dialogue scenes meant to be presented on a big proscenium stage (like *Oklahoma!*); through-sung pieces like operas; or revue-style cabaret shows with perhaps a unifying theme but little or no plot line (*Pump Boys & Dinettes,* for example). Keep in mind that the style also influences the sound— rock, rap, hip-hop, classical, standard Broadway, etc.—and therefore influences your choice of composer. (You may even want to think about this point earlier in the writing process.)

6. *Study the genre.* Once you have a direction for the style, research other musicals written in that same style. Read the scripts, listen to the recordings, and try to absorb their atmosphere. It is also useful to compare the original script of a play that's been turned into a musical with the musical's book—*The Four-Poster* with *I Do! I Do!, The Match-maker* with *Hello, Dolly!,* or even the comic strip of *Little Orphan Annie* with the libretto of *Annie*—to see how those writers approached it.

7. *Think musically.* In a musical, the most important element obviously is the music! More than words, it is the theatrical engine, the emotional drive of your show. You must trust it to tell the bulk of your story. In the early days of the American musical, plot was practically irrelevant. Bookwriters were told, "Just give me the gozintas and gozoutas," meaning the spoken line that "goes into" and "goes out of" the songs. Remember, too, that your beautifully crafted monologues and even much of your dialogue may be turned into songs, so try not to become too attached to them. You have to love music, surrender to it, and know how to direct its flow. If you are loathe to give up your carefully crafted words and don't want to embrace and use musical energy, you are really better off sticking to straight plays, where words reign supreme.

8. *Play with rhythms.* Once you are comfortable using music as your through-line, check the overall rhythm of your piece. Are you placing too many ballads close together? Do you have solos alternating with ensembles, duets, trios? Don't forget to check the internal structure of the scenes themselves as well. Often, playwrights-turning-librettists fall into the trap of scenes all being identically structured: talk, talk, talk, sing; talk, talk, talk, sing. The songs should be so woven into the plot that they highlight the emotional moments, drive the action, and

occasionally comment on it (in specialty material like comedy numbers). It's also important to vary the placement of musical numbers. In musicals, dialogue should be thought of as the shortest distance between two songs.

9. *Use special options.* Musicals have their own unique vocabulary. Creative possibilities abound. For instance, you can make use of dance or mime to instrumental underscoring to tell part of your story. You also might consider condensing several transitional scenes into one large musical number. Musical reprises at key emotional moments are very effective devices. You have to begin thinking musically and dramatically.

10. *Have fun.* Writing a musical is a huge undertaking. Mounting even the small ones can be costly and risky. The road to success, especially in today's theatrical market, is paved with potholes. That's why it is so important, from the outset, to love your material, feel comfortable with your collaborators, and enjoy every moment you can in the creative process. Keep in mind the true pot of gold at the end of the rainbow: the unmatched moment of sitting in a theater surrounded by an audience totally enthralled by the musical and dramatic spell you and your partners have woven.

[For more on this subject, the editors recommend *Writing the Broadway Musical*, by Aaron Frankel, published by Da Capo Press (ISBN 0-306-80943-5).]

Since You Asked | *11*

For more than ten years, readers at theaters and schools throughout the nation wrote to us with a myriad of questions on almost every conceivable aspect of theater craft. They wanted help, advice, and tips on specific situations that had arisen in their companies and departments. They wanted practical guidance they couldn't find elsewhere, which was what the *Stage Directions* department called "The Answer Box" gave them.

Rights and Wrongs

Q: When purchasing the rights to a play/musical, exactly what is included in the rights? Can a group duplicate the show logo from the Broadway production or must they come up with their own designs for program covers, tee shirts, etc.? And to what degree are "cuts" in dialogue permitted by rights purchase if any—for example, deleting foul language written in a play?

A: All rights—aside from basic copyright law—should be spelled out in the contract, including the use of logos. For example, the contract for *You're a Good Man, Charlie Brown* clearly states that "The Licensee agrees it will not use or reproduce the likenesses of any of the *Peanuts* comic-strip characters for advertising the play or for any other purpose."

In recent years, some producers have cagily copyrighted their show logo—*Annie*, for example—which means it cannot be used without permission. You can tell these by the (c) mark next to the logo, or in a statement in fine print somewhere else on the title page or reverse title page of the script (or on the cover of the cast record-ing, in the case of a musical). However, we do not advise using the logo of any show without first consulting the royalty house that han-dles the rights.

Regarding cuts in a script, some playwrights specify their condi-tions in the printed script—usually a warning on the reverse of the title page such as this one from *Me and My Girl*: "No changes shall be made in the play for the purpose of your production unless authorized in writing." Not all plays show such wording, but the lack of a warn-ing is no guarantee that cuts are allowed. Again, check with the pub-lisher or royalty house.

Baker's Plays does its customers a service by printing the following notice in its catalogue: "There are a number of playwrights who do not allow cuttings of their plays. There are a number of playwrights who allow cuttings only when a full act of their play is performed—no revi-sions, deletions, or piecing together to make a cutting. You must get in writing permission to perform any cutting [of any show] listed in our catalogue."

This pretty well sums up our advice as well.

Q: Do you have any tips on making videotapes of our musical pro-ductions?

A: We have: don't. Copyright law gives authors the exclusive right to control the reproduction of their work. When a publisher/agent grants you a license for your live stage production of a show, that license does not include the right to tape it because the authors retain the sole right to decide when or if their work is recorded in any way.

Live production rights are called *grand rights*. To record a show in any way requires *mechanical rights*, and most publisher/agents are not authorized to grant these to you. Even a videotape made for classroom use, as a personal memento, or as an archival record vio-lates the authors' separate right to reproduce their work. In many cases, the authors already have granted such rights exclusively to film or television companies, in which case you also would be infringing upon the rights granted by the authors to a third party. If caught, you or your organization are subject to healthy fines and other legal action.

Q: What materials do we get to put on the show?

A: This depends on which company you deal with. Some ask you to buy scripts, but rent the piano and orchestra parts. Others rent you both scripts and scores. In general, however, materials may include the following:

■ the script (the libretto or, when combined with the vocal parts, a libretto/vocal book)

■ the piano/vocal score (the piano part and all of the vocal lines)

■ the piano/conductor score (which includes cues from the show's orchestration for a conductor who also may be playing the keyboard part)

■ the full score (in which all the orchestra parts are arranged on the page for the conductor's reference)

■ the orchestra parts (individual instrumental books for each musician in the pit orchestra)

These materials are usually sent to you six to eight weeks before the show opens, depending on the publisher/agent. Make sure you clarify this when requesting a show for production; if you need materials earlier, most companies will oblige, although in some cases they may assess an additional fee.

DIRECTING THE MUSICAL

How to Provide the Guiding Vision

D irectors are the unseen presence in musical stage
productions, yet their influence is everywhere to be
seen—and heard.

As we point out in *The Stage Directions Guide to
Directing*, the director of a stage production is like the captain
of a ship, and the director is always on watch to make sure the
vessel reaches its destination. There are many workers below
decks, each with his or her own task, but it's ultimately the
captain's role to meld these people into a successful team.
And, like the audience in a theater, the ship's passengers seldom see the hard work that goes on behind the scenes,
because the emphasis is always on helping them enjoy the
voyage.

And all of that is especially true of the musical, which is
the most collaborative of all the performing arts. Musical theater has an immense following and brings with it special challenges for the director. Each musical voyage is different—a
different work, a different audience, a different cast, a different
interpretation. And since each voyage is different, there's no
one way to run this particular ship.

However, there are many ideas and tools that you, as
director, can use to shape the musical production, many of
which you'll find in this section. We also refer you to *The Stage
Directions Guide to Directing* and *The Stage Directions Guide to
Auditions* for additional ideas and tips.

12 | "Putting It Together"

The Musical as Collaborative Art

What makes a good director? Because the director is in charge of the production, there is a great need for a strong overview of theater. Any effective director needs knowledge or experience in acting, stagecraft, lighting, costuming, makeup, theater history, dance and stage movement, and psychology. In addition, the director of a musical needs to understand the essentials of this particular art form.

As a director, you typically are responsible for staging the play, coaching the performers, and making sure all the elements of the production, including music and dancing, are integrated. To ensure artistic unity, the director must be the final authority in all matters related to the production. But "authority" does not mean being a dictator. It means that you develop a unified artistic vision of the show, that you communicate it clearly with your production staff and actors, and that you allow them to find creative methods of supporting that vision. "Final authority" really means that if there are questions of appropriateness that cannot be resolved without the director, the director will make the final determination.

Other members of a production team include a technical director, lighting designer, costume designer, set designer, and stage manager. Some teams also include a makeup designer; property head; and crew chiefs for stage, lighting, makeup, sound, house, and publicity. Most important in musical theater, your team ideally also will include a choreographer and musical director.

To make sure the team proceeds with its work effectively, you'll need to have preproduction meetings to share your vision of the show, determine the budget, ensure that rights to the play are cleared, the theater is booked, and schedule a series of conferences with production staff members. You'll also want to set the dates and times for auditions. (For more on this subject, see *The Stage Directions Guide to Auditions*.)

The director takes the lead at the first production conference. Here, you present your interpretation of the musical and your concept of the production's style or look. The designers, choreographer, and musical director will have a chance to react to your ideas, enlarge on them, or even suggest a different approach. Listen carefully. Their ideas may alter the way you see the play. On the other hand, if you decide to proceed with your original concept, try to incorporate as much as possible the best ideas of your staff.

A second conference is called after your collaborators have had a chance to mull over the ideas expressed at the first meeting. Preliminary sketches of sets, costumes, and lighting designs are presented and discussed to see how they mesh with the director's and choreographer's vision and how they support each other.

A third meeting looks at revised designs, color sketches, and scale models of the sets. The choreographer needs to be present to see if any of the designs conflict with practical concerns of stage movement. At this point, all involved should have a good sense of what the show will look like so they can continue to refine their concepts and designs.

The director should continue to confer with technical staff throughout the production period. However, these conferences should be completed by the start of rehearsal, so the director can concentrate on working with the performers.

Clearly, in a musical, much of the rehearsal time will be in the hands of the musical director and choreographer. The importance of music and dance cannot be overlooked in the success of a musical, and a good director listens carefully to the ideas and suggestions of those colleagues. However, dance routines or musical interpretations that do not support the director's approach to the show can damage the production. The director is always the ultimate authority.

Previously we asked, "What makes a good director?" Aside from training, good instincts, intelligence, and organization, a director must be able to create an artistic vision of the show and then communicate that vision effectively to cast and production staff. It's a tall order, but it's done every day.

13 | "It's Not Where You Start (It's Where You Finish)"

The Power of Transformation

There are many elements important to understand for those directing—or for that matter, producing or performing—in a musical. But there is one underlying fact that drives everything else in this form of theater. Musical theater is about transformation, usually a change in the essential personality of one or more of the main characters. Sometimes we refer to musical theater story lines as Cinderella stories or fairy tales. There is some truth in that observation, but there is much more at work.

Musical theater aims directly at something within us that wants desperately to believe that there is hope, that goodness can prevail, that love will conquer all. Thus, the basic shape of a musical is almost always the same. We are introduced to a character or characters to whom we quickly take a liking. However, they find themselves in a difficult situation that must be resolved for them to be happy. In many cases, the focus is a man and a woman who have the potential for genuine affection toward each other, but who are kept apart by internal or external forces. By the end of the show, these people have been transformed and can find happiness.

Thus, in *My Fair Lady*, we have the mismatched Eliza Dolittle and Professor Henry Higgins. By play's end, she has risen to meet him on his own terms, and he has acknowledged his dependence on another human being.

In *Annie*, everything seems stacked against the little orphan girl, and while Annie herself never really changes, she is a catalyst for change in the lives of everyone else. By the final curtain, she has the family she deserves and those who have helped her are rewarded, as well—and those who have tran-spired against her are punished.

In *Fiddler on the Roof*, Tevye is a very different man at the end than he is at the beginning. He learns that love is more important than the traditions on which he and his people have built their lives. In the show's final moments, as he and the remnants of his family leave their homeland, it is clear that it's the strength of that love that will sustain them all.

Growth and Contrast

This concept of transformation underpins everything in a musical production, so it is vital that the director and everyone else involved understand it as well.

As director, you lead off with your own study of the libretto. Note the position or mental state of the main characters at the end of the show, and contrast this with their situation at the beginning. Then you need to find the hints of character change throughout the show; these need special attention so the audience accepts the change at show's end.

It's especially important when the character could seem unpleas-ant in some way. For example, Henry Higgins may be self-centered and insufferable, but he cannot be seen as cruel. Cruelty implies plea-sure at hurting others, but Higgins is not even aware that he is hurting anyone. And that is the comic point: he thinks everyone else is the problem, not himself. From his perspective, he is perfectly reasonable and totally independent of any messy romantic inclinations, as is clear in his song, "An Ordinary Man."

But by the final curtain, Eliza has shown him that he is not perfect and self-contained, and that human companionship (it may be too much to call it romantic love) is important. Eliza respects him for his learning and his abilities, and chastises him for his selfishness in the song "Without You," which also signals her independence from him. Higgins works through his subsequent emotions in "I've Grown Accustomed to Her Face," in which he, at last, admits that another person is important in his life.

Similarly, in *Oklahoma!*, Curly is a bit too sure of himself, and Lau-rey has a quick temper that gets her into trouble. But the director and actors must be careful never to let the audience dislike these two char-acters. Their behavior may be immature, but the two will mature as events unfold. The same is true for Nellie Forbush, Billy Bigelow, Dolly Levi, Anna Leonowens, and many other musical-theater characters who could appear less than sympathetic if their character faults over-power their good points.

Even when a character has no apparent character flaws, the director must work with the performer to underscore the change that will take place—and to keep the characterization from being on one note throughout. For example, *West Side Story*'s Maria must make a believable transition from a naïve young woman to the confident person who confronts the gang members at the end of the show. And we must feel that Dolly Levi has some motive for marrying Horace Vandergelder other than his money.

Each musical presents its own set of circumstances and its own challenges for the director. However, it's our experience that a unifying vision of the show is important to all who work on it. One way to supply that vision is to look for the elements of transformation and keep them firmly in mind as you shape the show or your characterization.

"Have You Heard?" 14

For a good musical production, a director needs good performers. To get good performers, you need good auditions. For good auditions, you need to get out good information.

Let Them Know What You Want

A good audition serves the common interest of both director and performer; both want the auditions to go smoothly. The director wants to cast the show and the actors want to be cast. The director wants the actors to do their best, and so do they.

So, as a director, how do you get the right people to audition, and to audition well? Aside from issues over which you have no control (the pool of singing, dancing, and acting talent in your area, for example), the simplest answer is to provide all the information the performers need to prepare and perform well and to understand the commitment they must make to the show.

Audition announcements are standard operating procedure. However, in too many cases, the announcement are bare bones at best. If you want to get the right people to auditions, you need to spell out what you expect. That's especially true for a musical, where specific singing and dancing skills may be needed. A good audition announcement does more than give time, location, and the name of the show. Indeed, the more information you can share with auditioners, the better.

On the other hand, you don't want to overwhelm people. Perhaps the best way is to present a brief outline of essential audition information in the announcement, and then make available a more complete set of information in the form of an audition packet, available before or during auditions.

The Announcement

The announcement itself should have the following information: name of production, playwright name, name of director,

production dates, audition dates and times, list of characters (including gender and age), and a brief description of the audition setup (for
example, cold or prepared readings, whether scripts are available
beforehand, and whether performers may audition with a song from
the show). Make sure there is a contact name and phone number, as
well as the address of the rehearsal location and a place or contact
for the audition packet.

Here is an excerpt from the audition announcement for the Theatre Charlotte production of *Follies*:

> *Follies* is a haunting memory piece that takes place on the stage
> of a decaying old theater, to which a number of retired *Follies*
> performers have been invited for a final reunion before the the-
> ater is demolished. A ghostly aura surrounds these grand old
> ladies and gents as they revive their glittery old routines while
> rekindling friendship, rivalry, romance, and betrayal.
>
> Filled with memory, illusions, and disillusions of love, this
> lavish musical weaves lyrics, music, costumes, and choreogra-
> phy into an elegant tapestry of theater nostalgia. The winner of
> seven Tony Awards, *Follies* features a sophisticated and pene-
> trating score by Stephen Sondheim. In addition to director Keith
> Martin and designer Vernon Carroll, *Follies* will feature guest art-
> ists John Coffey as musical director and Ron Chisholm (who
> appeared in the national tour of *Follies*) as choreographer. Roles
> are available for twenty-three men and twenty-five women from
> teenage through seventy. The pre-audition workshop will be
> held at 7:30 P.M. on Monday, July 10. Auditions will be held at
> 7:30 P.M. on Monday and Tuesday, July 24 and 25. Scripts are
> available for overnight checkout; a $25 deposit is required. Per-
> formance dates are September 14 through October 1.

The Packet

Because the audition announcement is widely distributed, it is typically on one sheet of paper to keep the cost down. However, for those
who want to know more about the show and the production envi-
sioned by the director, an audition packet contains all the previous
information, but in significantly greater detail. Let's take a look at the
packet, which may contain four to eight or more pages of information.

■ *Time commitment.* Make sure you include when rehearsal starts
and what days/times are included; complete production dates and
times (don't forget to include pickup rehearsals, if you plan to have
them). This will give actors a chance to see if they have time conflicts.

■ *The show itself.* Begin with a description and synopsis of the show, particularly if it's not well known. A few sentences on the author are helpful, as are comments on the musical's literary, social, or historical importance, and any awards or critical acclaim it may have received. Explain the type of music the show contains and the type of voices or performers needed to put it across.

■ *Character and voice-range breakdown.* List all the characters, including name, age, physical and emotional characteristics, relationship to other characters, vocal range, dance requirements, and other and special requirements as appropriate.

■ *The director's vision.* To be familiar with a show is helpful to the actor, but so is the vision the director brings to this particular production. You might explain why you want to do this show, what about it attracts you. Also take time to give a sense of the particular style or approach you intend to use.

■ *The audition process.* Make it clear whether you intend to use cold readings or prepare a reading or monologue in advance. If you do not want people auditioning with a song from the show being cast, say so. However, you might suggest the type of song that would be helpful, such as other songs by the same composer or from the same era or style. (You always can have auditioners stay after singing and run them up or down the scale to determine their range.) Be as explicit as possible. Actors will appreciate it, and you'll have to answer fewer questions during the audition. In addition to giving the time and place of the audition, you might suggest that everyone arrive at the start, in order to hear what others are doing or to allow you to begin grouping people in readings immediately. If the audition is by appointment only, make it clear how long before the appointed time the actors may arrive and where they should wait. Put yourself in the actors' place and consider all the questions they might have. Then answer them.

■ *Scripts, scenes, and scores.* Making scripts and scores (or selected scenes and songs) available beforehand is beneficial to the actors and to an efficient audition process. Cold readings are not always avoidable, but they almost always are less satisfactory for both actor and director than a prepared audition. If you don't want (or can't afford) to make multiple copies available, ask if your local library will put several on reserve—available to check out for a limited time. (Note that in the example from Theatre Charlotte, scripts can be checked out from the theater, but are secured by a $25 deposit.) Having the score available for checkout also is helpful to those who can read music because they quickly can determine if a part is within their range; if they can't read music, they may have a friend or teacher who can.

■ *A little history.* A bit of explanation about your theater company helps place the production in perspective. This also is a good place to underscore basic virtues like respect, cooperation, and teamwork.

The entire packet should be printed double-sided (saves paper) and stapled at the top left corner to keep everything together. If you have an audition form that is customarily filled out at the audition itself, you might consider including it in the packet. That way people already have done this bit of work before they arrive.

The packet also should contain all pertinent contact information in case someone has a question or concern that needs to be addressed before the audition. Put it all together and you'll find that you and your performers will be more "together" as well.

"A Simple Little System" 15

The Eight Basics of Directing the Musical

STEPHEN PEITHMAN

P erhaps the greatest misunderstanding about musicals is that they are merely plays with music added. It's also the greatest danger for, if you believe it, you are setting yourself up for problems. In fact, the musical is its own theatrical form, as we noted previously, and in addition to all the standard requirements, it demands its own directorial approach.

If you are directing a musical for the first time or do so only occasionally, consider the following suggestions. They come from thirty years of observations as a director, performer, and student of musical theater.

Choose Carefully

If this is your first musical, consider one with the fewest technical demands, a small-to-medium cast, and a relatively simple structure (like *Once upon a Mattress* or *You're a Good Man, Charlie Brown*). That way, you can get comfortable with the form without overtaxing yourself or your resources.

Novice or not, don't take on a show unless you genuinely like or appreciate it. The musical is a fragile construct, and if you don't believe in the show, neither will the actors or the audience. If you don't already have a copy, by all means get Peter Filichia's *Let's Put on a Musical!*, which has much helpful information on choosing the right show for your situation.

Play to Your Strengths

Focus on what you do well and delegate the rest. Some directors are better at working with small groups or individual actors. Unfortunately, most musicals are not small. You will find that much of your time may be spent working with the ensemble because it needs the most work—and in musicals, the big picture is important.

If you find that moving herds of people around stage is unpleasant, enlist a choreographer to help you. Even if a song isn't choreographed in any usual sense of the word, good stage movement is important, and most choreographers seem to thrive on working with groups. If you don't have a choreographer available, try enlisting an assistant director. Either way, this will free you to concentrate on other aspects of the show. At the very least, have someone you trust come in and view the show during rehearsal in order to give you some perspective on how things look.

Plan Carefully

Musicals take more organization than plays because there are more pieces involved, and usually more people. On top of whatever else a play may demand, there is music to be learned and dances to be choreographed. Rehearsals will be more complicated too, because actors who have learned their music suddenly forget it when asked to dance at the same time (and vice versa).

It takes a lot longer to stage a musical number than a straight scene. More important, musical numbers take longer to say the same thing as spoken dialogue. They must sustain mood and character over a longer period of time. But, unlike a play, you can't ask the actors to speed up (or slow down) the dialogue, change pitch, or turn upstage. Musicals are more apt to be presentational; therefore, staging means reblocking, adjusting the volume of singers and orchestra, and struggling with music cues.

So, plan realistically for enough rehearsal time. Unlike a play, you won't have the performers all to yourself. In most cases a musical director will need time to work with them on songs, and a choreographer will want time to stage dance numbers.

Six weeks is a minimum rehearsal time if you rehearse five days a week; if it's your first show, add a week or two to be safe. The larger the cast or the more complex the technical demands, the longer the rehearsal period needs to be.

It's better to allow too much time than too little; you'll cheer up the cast (and yourself) if you announce a night off because things are going so well.

Keep It Simple

Keep your direction simple. Fussy details impede the momentum of the well-constructed musical. As it turns out, most shows are rather simplistic in their presentation of ideas—even *Fiddler on the Roof* and *West Side Story*. That's because so much of the time is spent singing and dancing that ideas (and plot) must be presented cleanly and simply. Unfortunately, many novice directors think they have to produce flash and glitter—a parade of big production numbers that brings down the house. You'll find you'll get better audience response if you parcel out the big moments so they stand out by comparison with the rest of the show.

Emphasize Character

Pay attention to character and pacing, for these are the two elements that can make or break your production.

Work with your performers to create strong characterizations—most musicals don't spend a lot of time in developing characters; they spring fully blown, as recognizable types (and sometimes stereotypes). This is a kind of theatrical shorthand that strikes some people as shallowness, but could just as easily be called efficiency.

However, if musical-comedy characters tend to be types, they cannot be played well without empathy. One of our editors recently saw a community-theater production of *Guys and Dolls* that was excellent in almost every respect. But the director (or perhaps the actress) had misjudged Sarah Brown as being only prim and repressed. Certainly, the joke is that Sky Masterson must talk this reserved young woman into flying to Havana with him. But for Sky to fall in love with her, there must be some fire underneath the facade. This was missing in the actress's portrayal, leaving the audience to wonder just what Sky Masterson saw in her.

Shakespearean director Jack Lynn says he always looks for the dramatic moments in a comedy to emphasize for contrast; that way the comedy is made even funnier.

"When I read a play for the first time, I go through it looking for places where I can ask the characters to play against the obviousness of the text, so that the thing has a dimension and can still be believable," Lynn says.

Thus, *Kiss Me, Kate*'s Lilli Vanessi and Fred Graham are more than merely overinflated egos. Those egos can be seen as defense mechanisms rooted in deep insecurities. We still can laugh at their excesses, but if the actors also portray the insecurities as well, we feel closer to Fred and Lilli as human beings.

Keep It Moving

Pacing is vital to the musical for several reasons. First, musicals are constructed as song-dialogue-song-dialogue. Yet, you must avoid any sense of things coming to a halt when a musical number ends—or worse, of the play coming to a halt when a song begins. Work toward a seamless flow.

Because musicals tend to be more episodic than straight plays, that flow is sometimes harder to maintain. Some shows are simply better than others in this respect. *The Unsinkable Molly Brown* is a particular problem, with scenes in widely flung locales and covering a period of many years. On the other hand, *Oklahoma!* takes place in one locale within a very short period of time.

Most musicals use the first act to introduce the characters, set up the situation, and create a conflict, with a crisis point typically placed just before the first-act curtain. The second act is usually shorter and focuses on resolving the conflict. Thus, pacing is most crucial in the first act; in most cases, the second-act momentum is built in. You'll need to work at getting the show moving from the first moment.

Avoid the Hollywood Trap

It's hard, but try not to let film versions scare or influence you. You're putting on a stage production, after all. Don't try to copy the film; you'll only look bad by comparison. Instead, work to create a unique look and feel that your audience will appreciate on its own merits.

Happily Ever After

Musicals are fairy tales. They tell us what we want to believe—that most people are good, that bad people are punished, that life is worth living. With very few exceptions (*Evita* is one), they're supposed to send people away feeling happy, satisfied that all loose ends have been tied up. People go to musicals to be entertained. The one great secret to a successful musical is that none of the hard work should show. The audience wants to relax and enjoy itself. If the audience senses you laboring, the illusion is destroyed. If you maintain the illusion, they will leave the theater feeling you have done a good job. And they'll be right.

"Keep A-Hoppin'"
In Musicals, Pacing Is Key

One of the most common faults in musical productions is that the pace tends to drag. The reason is simple: three different media—speech, dance, and song—are being combined in different ways and each makes strong demands on the performers.

Assuming you have escaped the curse of the triple-threat performer—can't sing, can't dance, can't act—it's still true that a wonderful vocalist may be a poor dancer or stilted in dialogue delivery. So, how does a director work with the cast to combine the three basic elements to create an all-around entertainment?

First, know where each performer's strength lies and shape the production accordingly. For example, avoid long dance routines with inexperienced performers, especially when singing or complex action follows.

Second, try to achieve a balance in your staging so the performer's strongest area emerges as such and any weaker areas are played down. The actor who can't move and sing at the same time might be blocked to begin his song seated in a chair, then moved to a new position in the interlude between verses.

Third, identify the flagging scenes and run them as isolated sequences, simplifying where necessary and emphasizing to the cast the importance of keeping the sequence moving. It's a good idea to have three or four rehearsals set aside for fixing problems. Then, during rehearsal, you can make notes of which things need to be worked on. Look particularly at your stage groupings; poor contact between performers often slows scenes down.

Last, dialogue scenes are often the weakest point of musical productions because they get too little rehearsal. It's tempting to push hardest on the musical numbers, but these do have a certain amount of momentum on their own. Once the music stops there is nothing to drive a scene forward except the energy the actors bring to it. Be sure to schedule enough time for dialogue scenes and don't be fooled into thinking your performers are principally singers and dancers. Even if true, this is exactly why they need more, not less, dialogue work.

17 | "So Many People"

As mentioned previously, one of the unique challenges of directing a musical is the simple problem of how to move around so many people. Here are some ideas about dealing with those big ensembles.

Large Casts, Small Groups

M ost musicals call for a large group on stage at some point. Indeed, you may have picked a show because it gives a large number of people a chance to be on stage.

However, as a director, you may find that you haven't enough time to spend in developing characterization for each member of the ensemble. One approach is to use an assistant director or choreographer to work with those people, someone who understands your vision for the production and can translate it for members of the group. Asking each member of the crowd to develop his or her own character is risky unless the actors are experienced.

A better way is to gather the group together, explain the show, the historical period, the essential action, your concept and plan for the show, and how the ensemble fits into this. Next, let the ensemble split up into smaller groups of six to eight people. Let the actors within each group discuss their characterizations. Allow them to invent a history for their character, personality quirks, and so on. Make sure each person in the group understands what the others are planning, then have them stand near each other on stage so they can interact appropriately. For example, if one actor decides to be hard of hearing, another can help by talking (or singing) into his ear.

Stanislavski once said that "there are no small parts, only small actors," and it's true. Everyone on stage is in full view of the audience, and it takes only one person out of character to distract from a scene. The surest way to invite ruin is to let a crowd ad lib on stage without some guidance.

Remember that the appearance of spontaneity is enough. If the play takes place in an historical setting, the actors should know enough not to say "Wow!," for example. Decide what the appropriate ad libs might be and stick with them. (Some directors insist that a crowd should murmur something like "rhubarb" when conversing among themselves. The idea is to give the illusion of speech without anything too specific that might distract from the main action.)

Members of groups or choruses sometimes must be reminded that they are not normally the main object of interest on stage. A director should explain the focus of each scene and how the group can help the audience focus as well. Often this means grouping crowds appropriately or minimizing their movement. Keep minor characters around the periphery of the stage whenever possible. If the audience is supposed to be watching someone on stage, it usually helps if the chorus is focused on that person, too. If that isn't possible—such as when Amalia and Georg converse in a crowded restaurant in *She Loves Me*—lower the lighting on the stage except for the principals. If lighting levels can't be adjusted, put the leading player farther downstage or on a higher level than the crowd. Or have the crowd sit on the ground or in chairs while the principals stand.

Finally, have an assistant watch for the common failings of chorus members, such as anticipating the reaction to a particular line. (In their enthusiasm, inexperienced actors often vocalize excitement or disappointment a fraction before the speech that is supposed to motivate them.)

And remember, most members of the chorus or crowd actually enjoy getting notes from the director—it makes them feel important.

Crowd Scenes Made Easy

Instead of blocking each member of the crowd separately, try this trick. First divide people into groups (Group A, B, C, etc.). Then give one set of entrances and exits: "Group A comes in through the stage left door, Group B down the center rear steps, and Group C from stage right around the rocks."

Next, unless the group is a mob and acting with one mind, assign character and motivation in subgroups. For example, you might want one or two people in each group to be very verbal, another two to use extravagant gestures, some others to be bored with the action, and so on.

In other words, go for the big picture. Once this is established, encourage the actors to add business where appropriate. The advantage is that you save time and effort, while also projecting the image of an organized director who knows what he or she wants. And that is worth something all by itself.

18 | "It's the Little Things You Do Together"

Of course, not every show has a large cast with people everywhere. And that can mean a different order of problem—and a different kind of solution.

Big Show, Small Cast

SCOTT MILLER

The company I work with is a small, alternative musical-theater group, so we don't get the great number of people at auditions other companies might get for *Godspell* or *The Music Man*. There have been times when this has been a real problem for us, but with a production of *Pippin*, we learned this problem could be turned into an advantage.

At our auditions, only about twenty-five people showed up, some of them, frankly, not very good. Needing seven leads and a chorus for *Pippin*, I didn't know how I was going to cast the show.

I decided I needed to look at the show fresh and forget what I knew about the Broadway production, the video version, and other productions I had seen. I had to unlearn everything I knew about doing a big musical, and ask myself some very basic questions. These were questions you might ask yourself any time you find yourself in the same situation.

First, is the musical in question "big" because the story demands it or because that's just the way everyone does it? Could the leads also be in the chorus, as with *A Chorus Line* and other concept musicals? Can we cast the same actor in more than one role without upsetting the show's premise? What would happen to the material if we did the show without a big chorus? Would that go against the creators' original intentions? And—perhaps most important—will the audience accept our choices if we don't match their preconceived notions of how this show should look?

In our case, we decided *Pippin* was a "big" musical only because that's the way most people do it. However, a closer look reveals that the cast is "a group of actors," according to the stage directions. "Their costumes are of an undetermined period. But they are definitely players . . . a troupe . . . a theatrical caravan of some kind." So, it made perfect sense for our own actors to play more than one part, to appear both as a lead and in the chorus.

Using a small cast would remind the audience that this was indeed a troupe of actors, not really Pippin's family, and that they were making this up as they went. Casting the same actor as both Charles and (in drag) his mother, Berthe, also reinforced the important concept that these people were only actors. With the major players all doubling as chorus members, we needed fewer people to fill out the cast. And it proved a lot more fun for the actors, who each now had several parts to play.

From this point, we began to explore related issues. Near the end of the play, Leading Player says to the audience, "We'll be there for you . . . waiting . . . anytime you want us. Why, we're right inside your heads." Clearly, the implication is that the Players are all in Pippin's mind—or our collective imagination. This premise gave us tremendous license; if everything in the show is an illusion, then is it possible to go too far? Treating the show as a hallucination allowed our unusual casting choices to make perfect sense.

We ended up casting only eleven actors in the show, since a *commedia dell'arte* traveling theater company probably would employ as few actors as possible who could play many roles, in order to keep costs down. Even when two of our eleven actors dropped out because of scheduling conflicts, I found this wasn't a problem. All the performers were strong actors and singers. And since the stage we perform on is tiny, even with only nine people it still looked pretty full for the group scenes.

Most important, the show's basic premise of a traveling troupe of players playing out Pippin's life for him seemed more real because our own troupe was small—everyone doubling parts, taking walk-on parts, participating in the orgy scene, and making only minor costume changes (a hat, a tunic, a mask, etc.) to change from one character to another. The audience enjoyed the joke of the same actor playing both Pippin's father and grandmother—without Pippin noticing the resemblance!

To maintain unity in the design elements, our casting demanded that our sets likewise be minimal and extremely versatile, which forced us to be creative and also ended up saving us lots of money.

Although I'd seen *Pippin* many times and have loved the show for years, suddenly it seemed new again, without actually having changed the material at all. It wasn't the same show everyone else has done, which allowed those of us who knew the show to appreciate once again what first made us love the material. The audience, too, felt like it was seeing the show for the first time. Our re-invention impressed many people enough that they continue to attend our productions just to see how we'll approach familiar material.

I must emphasize again that our audiences accepted the show's new look because it made sense. We changed nothing simply for the sake of change. Instead, we simplified, eliminating the clutter of spectacle, allowing what we thought was the essence of the show to shine through. What we discovered could apply to dozens of other musicals.

After all, at its core, the best theater isn't about crowds, special effects, or big sets. It's about people.

"Side by Side by Side" | 19

Using Directorial Shorthand

Subdividing a stage into discrete playing areas can make life easier when directing a musical—with a big cast or a small one. Better yet, it actually can improve the stage picture and lighting as well.

Communication between director and actor is improved because the director can say, "Littlechap walks from 7 to 5, pauses, and moves to the table in 3." If the stage were divided along the lines of the following diagram, this translates as "Littlechap enters upstage right, walks center stage, pauses, and then moves to the table downstage left."

9	8	7
6	5	4
3	2	1

[audience]

Many actors, especially inexperienced ones, find it useful to imagine the stage as a giant tic-tac-toe board instead of memorizing the upstage/downstage/stage right/stage left configuration.

Such a setup also helps your lighting designer. With the acting areas divided into sections, the lighting of each area can be carefully controlled. It also allows for continuity, so that an actor can move from area to area and remain well lighted.

The reference to "Littlechap" stems from our observation of this system used in a production of *Stop the World—I Want to Get Off*. Using a bare stage, the director was able to provide dynamic blocking for the cast that filled the entire playing area. At the same time, individual squares could be lighted for more intimate moments, or to emphasize the return to a specific location mentioned in the script. For example, Littlechap goes into his boss's office several times during the musical. This was always placed in Square 4 and always lighted in the same way.

Areas should not be too small or they become difficult to light and their location confusing to the actors. On the other hand, if the areas are too large, lighting them well may be difficult and again, their boundaries won't be clear.

If the diagram shown is of a stage area 24 by 24 feet, each of the nine sections would be 8-foot square. This is about right for both acting and lighting purposes.

"Finishing the Hat" 20

You made it to almost all the way. Your directorial efforts are looking good and your musical seems to be working. You've gotten to the end. Well, not quite. There's one more thing to do.

How to Design an Effective Curtain Call

STEPHEN PEITHMAN

*I*t's a pain to stage and often is left until the last possible moment. But your production's curtain call is far too important to be treated as an afterthought. On the contrary, it deserves the same creative thought and planning as the show that precedes it. After all, it is the final stage picture the audience sees before it leaves the theater.

It also signals the end of this particular theatergoing experience, acting as an important transition between the world of the musical and the real world to which the audience is returning. And, of course, it gives the audience a chance to show its appreciation for the performance as a whole, and to individual performers in particular.

Understanding these three elements is essential to creating an effective curtain call for a musical production. So are these five rules of thumb: keep it brief, keep it moving, keep it building to a climax, keep it interesting, then clear the stage. Here's how you can put these rules into action.

1. *Keep it building.* Generally speaking, the book dictates the order in which the performers appear, from the chorus to minor characters, from secondary characters to the leads. Often you'll find that during the course of rehearsal, the relative importance of characters to the production becomes clearer—a good reason for waiting to block bows until the last run-through before technical rehearsals.

Begin by grouping together all those with no lines or without distinguishing characters—the chorus in most musicals.

Next bring on the bit players—those with one or two lines or solos—again, as a group. If there is a dancer who steps out of the chorus to do a solo, this is the place to recognize him or her.

Follow with the supporting players, in groups of two, three, or four related characters. Then the lead players, giving each a solo bow, working toward the central character. If there are two central characters, as in *Kiss Me, Kate*, bring on the two actors together, then let each take a bow, first to the other, and then to the audience.

Finally, have the entire company take a bow, then acknowledge the conductor and orchestra, and close the curtain.

2. *Keep it moving.* Overlap all stage movement. An individual or group walks quickly downstage to receive applause, and as soon as they are in position and begin bowing, the next group or individual should begin its way down, and so on with each successive bow. This may take some rehearsal, but the result is worth it. The energy on stage will be matched by that of the audience.

Movement is especially important in a musical, where bows normally have their own music. A good musical director will have additional music ready, but it's better if the cast keeps on track. Rehearse bows to the music, so that actors know their cue. That way, if someone slows down, the next person can pick up the pace, knowing where his or her bow should begin in the score.

3. *Keep it interesting.* Creating an effective final picture means paying attention to how people are grouped on the stage.

Build the stage picture throughout the call, adding groups and levels from backstage to front. If there are platforms or stairs, place actors on them after they finish their bows. This not only adds variety to the picture, but also lets the audience see everyone on stage.

You also can use groups to underscore the ensemble nature of a show, even if you're building to a final solo bow, such as in *Hello, Dolly!* or *Mame.* Just design the curtain call so that the groupings gradually frame a downstage center position, into which the lead actor walks. (Make sure that the character merits this focus. Otherwise a sense of anticlimax will ruin the effect.)

The group bow at the end of the curtain call should be rehearsed so that everyone bows as one. The simplest method is to trigger it by someone in the front row who is visible to everyone on stage. This person begins by first tilting the head back slightly, so that when they bend forward, the rest of the cast is with them.

In a musical, the cast also should acknowledge the conductor, who then asks the orchestra to stand. The cast may join in the applause for the musicians, but it's simpler for them to extend arms toward the conductor and keep them there until the orchestra has been recognized. A final group bow should follow to reframe the stage picture.

4. *Get off the stage.* Keep curtain calls as brief as possible. The audience wants to acknowledge the performers, but it doesn't want to make a night of it. Besides, clapping for more than a few minutes is tiring. Even if the audience stamps, applauds, and continues to yell "Bravo!," fade the lights, drop the curtain, bring up the house lights, and go home. Leave them wanting more.

Curtainless Calls

Blocking most curtain calls is fairly straightforward. However, some situations present special challenges. For example, if your play is presented without a curtain, creating a stage picture must be done in full view of the audience. Even if the cast returns in a blackout, they can be seen getting into position.

In a production of *She Loves Me*, I had the lovers walk off the stage, arm in arm, followed by a slow fade except for a single street lamp illuminating the exterior of the parfumerie. As the lights came back up, the cast returned to the stage through the parfumerie door to accept the applause.

For *Once upon a Mattress*, I kept Winifred asleep in bed, with the returning cast forming a picture around her. Prince Dauntless made one last futile attempt to awaken her. Illuminated by a follow spot, she attempted to sit up, then sank back in sleep—too much applause (and laughter).

In each case, the curtain call's blocking was suggested by the set itself, providing a satisfying conclusion to the performance. Look to your own set for similar ideas when staging a curtainless call.

True to Life

In general, actors should take the curtain call as themselves, not as their characters. As a director once told me, "The play is over. The characters no longer exist."

Whatever your choice, make sure that all players appear either as themselves or in character—although the rule can be broken to good effect, as with the sleeping Winifred. In a production one of our editors saw recently, everyone took bows as themselves except for one actor. By staying in character, he seemed to be begging for attention. ("Hey, remember me? I'm the crusty old guy with the limp!")

Final Thoughts

1. *Keep the focus.* Audiences sometimes respond more to effort than artistry, and some players may receive a bigger hand than their work deserves. For example, a cute player can get a bigger hand than a more competent but restrained lead. And actresses who cry or die on stage often get more than their share of applause. Supporting players with flashy roles may get a bigger reaction than the leads. If you think that this may be the case in your production, and want to give everyone in the cast equal recognition, you can (a) present only a company bow; (b) block the cast into large groups of related characters and have each group take a bow together; or (c) put the audience favorite in a group of three feature players.

2. *Plan carefully.* Even spontaneous displays such as presenting flowers to the leading lady or calling the director on stage for a bow should be planned. In fact, prepare and rehearse anything that takes place within the existing curtain-call time.

3. *Stick to your guns.* Because of the obvious order of least important characters to most important, not everyone will be happy with their lot. Don't change the curtain call to placate an actor, however. Explain the order of the bows, perhaps, but let it go at that. And don't change the curtain call once it's blocked and set. The cast doesn't need new blocking after opening night.

4. *Put some teeth into it.* For some reason, many actors don't smile during bows. Perhaps it's modesty, perhaps it's fatigue. Whatever the reason, remind them to keep smiling. The audience wants to believe that everyone on stage has enjoyed themselves. Smiles encourage more applause, too.

MUSICAL DIRECTION AND CHOREOGRAPHY

PART IV

How to Keep Your Production Moving

*T*here is direction and then there is musical direction, because it's not called "musical" theater for nothing. As we've seen, the use of music—whether for singing or dancing—lies at the heart of your production. As a director, you will most likely be working with a musical director and choreographer. How well you work with them will have a great deal to do with the success of your show. And if you find yourself acting as both director and choreographer, you have even more on your plate.

In this section, we look at the basic elements of music and dance as they relate to creating a musical production.

21 | "I Feel a Song Coming On"

Comparing Notes with Two Musical Directors

HOPE S. BRESLAUER

You can't have a successful musical without a musical director, the person whose role is to take what is written on the sheets of staffs and guide how it flows from all instruments, including the human voice. Rodgers and Hammerstein can put the notes and lyrics on paper, but if the musical director doesn't execute them correctly, they are meaningless.

The musical director joins the creative process at the very beginning of any production, but his or her job can be quite different, depending on whether it's a Broadway musical or a regional one, an original score or a revival.

Broadway Style

According to Patrick Brady, the musical director of the 1999 Tony Award–winning musical *Fosse*, "A new musical requires long talks with the composer, because you are dealing with new orchestrations and new songs that have never been heard on stage before. With a revival, you get the score from the publisher, open it up, and find there is a lot less work. All you do is essentially hire the orchestra, cast the singers, and play what's written."

While *Fosse* was a new musical, it was unusual because the songs were all well known, compiled from Bob Fosse–choreographed stage musicals and films. Still, the transitions between numbers were all new tunes, composed by the musical director himself. Brady, who has worked on such shows as *Crazy for You*, *Triumph of Love*, and *The Will Rogers Follies*, says his main concern was to make the music sound as authentically Fosse-like as possible.

"I did a lot of research with musical supervisor Gordon Harrell, who had worked with Fosse on several shows," says

Brady. "I was mainly concerned that the tempo of the music and [choreography] remain as much like they were in the 1950s and 1960s as possible, and to give the music a modern touch, as Fosse would have liked it. We didn't want this to be a museum piece."

Once Brady and his collaborators decide what they want a show to sound like, the next job is to work with the performers to achieve and then maintain that sound. In a show like *Fosse*, there is a lot of give and take in the casting process, usually giving to dance and taking from voice. *Fosse* is, after all, 60 percent dance and 40 percent singing—a recent trend in musical theater.

"We did have some people in this show who weren't the best singers," admits Brady, "but because their dancing was so phenomenal, we (the musical director and choreographer) had to compromise. It's tricky, but I think the general level of singing is better in dancers today than it was twenty years ago."

After the show goes up, it's Brady's job to make sure the sound is as fresh a year later as it was on opening night. He does this by conducting six shows a week and making sure all understudies, who often have to fill in at a moment's notice, rehearse all elements of the show four hours a day, twice a week.

Way off Broadway

In most regional and community theaters, original shows are rarely performed, and runs of more than a month or so are less likely. Thus, putting on a musical in this type of venue involves a very different set of elements. For veteran musical director Paul Wiley, the job starts in a preproduction meeting where he sits down with the director and choreographer to figure out the challenges of the show they have chosen to stage. Unlike Broadway, where an orchestra is a given, Wiley has to ask if the budget even allows him to have one, and if so, how large it can be.

Next come the auditions, which Wiley admits is his least favorite part of the whole production. Though he always puts in his two cents' worth during the casting process, rarely does he win a fight. Ultimately, the director's vision prevails. Unfortunately, that may not always be to the musical advantage of that particular show.

"They will cast people who may not necessarily be able to sing the role," he explains. "I'll say what I have to say, because I don't ever want to be in the position of hearing 'Why didn't you tell me she couldn't hit that note?' I will always say someone can't sing it the way it's written, but if they insist on using that person, we work around it and come up with something else, musically."

Wiley, who has done musical directing for more than fifteen years, savors the rehearsal process and relishes working with a chorus. "In community theater, I think doing these musicals can really affect someone's life, because most people want to sing, even in the chorus," he says. His love for choral work is what made *Funny Girl* the most difficult show he has ever worked on.

"It's hard because so much of the show relies musically on one performer, and it's difficult to serve the songs well and not have them all sound the same," Wiley explains. "And it's a challenge to keep the ensemble's morale up in that show. The chorus doesn't have a lot to do, but they are so necessary. The audience is relieved when the ensemble comes on for a Ziegfeld number, because *Funny Girl* is such a long, serious show. I felt bad for the ensemble, who stood backstage so much of the time, because I was asking so much of them."

Once Wiley has got what he wants out of his cast, he finds the ultimate joy in seeing all elements mesh.

"My favorite part is when the orchestra and chorus finally get together. It's a joyous thing to see people on stage who never thought they'd be there, singing with an orchestra."

"The Sound of Music" 22

Resources Are There for the Finding

A s director or musical director, you want to know what the music sounds like beforehand so you can understand its shape and complexities, and choose the right show. Then you want to continue working on the right sound throughout rehearsals so it all comes together opening night.

Here are some resources to help you do exactly that.

Recordings

Most of us first hear a show's score on a recording, yet most of these are not complete. Recording companies try to fit everything on one CD or cassette, and in the process, jettison dance music or underscoring, which they feel is of little interest to most listeners.

However, for the past several years Jay Records has been recording complete two-CD sets with all the music, including dance and dialogue underscoring for such shows as *Sweet Charity, Annie Get Your Gun, Guys and Dolls, The King and I, Kiss Me, Kate, My Fair Lady, South Pacific*, and many more, all in their original orchestrations and keys. These recordings are made with top-flight Broadway performers, and are well worth a listen.

Jay has a website, <www.jayrecords.com>, with a complete description of each recording in its catalogue. It does not sell recordings itself, but you can buy them by special order through your local record store or via one of the many online book and recording websites.

Accompaniment

Finding a good rehearsal accompanist can be a problem. It's tedious work, yet requires a fine musician with patience and a strong sense of humor. A number of play publishers—including Eldridge, I.E. Clark, and Pioneer Drama Service—offer cassettes for rehearsal and, in some cases, for performance. Inquire about such services when you deal with any play publisher; if it doesn't currently offer taped accompaniment, perhaps greater demand will encourage more to do so.

A step beyond cassettes is Music Theatre International's RehearScore, a computerized rehearsal pianist/musical director's aide. This easy-to-use program consists of two parts (the RehearScore Songfile and the RehearScore sequencer program), and is available with your performance license for an additional $200 for the entire rental period.

Each RehearScore Songfile is a complete rendition of the piano/conductor score on a computer disk, recorded and programmed by a professional pianist and, whenever possible, edited by the composer. The Songfile, available for both IBM PC and Macintosh, includes the entire piano/conductor score with the piano part, any orchestral cues, and each vocal line on its own track. Every musical number, including scene change, dance, and underscore music, is recorded in its entirety. You can change tempo for the learning of dance routines, or play only certain vocal lines, and make recordings for cast members to take with them for at-home rehearsal, and so on.

For the RehearScore Songfile PC users need a MIDI interface or interface card (such as the Roland MPU-401), a sequencer program (such as Master Tracks, Sequencer Plus, or CakeWalk), and a synthesizer. (General MIDI synthesizers are often the least expensive, and have preset channels to automatically play the correct instrument sounds. Many have a built-in MIDI interface that connects the synthesizer directly to your computer's serial port. They often come bundled with a sequencer program.)

Macintosh users need a MIDI interface (available from Music Theatre International with your rental) and a synthesizer. (Many general MIDI synthesizers have a built-in MIDI interface that connects the synthesizer directly to your Mac's modem port using a standard serial cable.)

Music Theatre International has RehearScore for most of its most popular shows, including *Annie, Company, Damn Yankees, Evita, The Fantasticks, Fiddler on the Roof, Guys and Dolls, Into the Woods,* and *West Side Story.* (Music Theatre International; 421 W. 54th St., New York, NY 10019; 212/541-4684)

"The Music That Makes Me Dance"

Putting the Orchestra on Stage

STEPHEN PEITHMAN

23

T here is something so theatrical about a musical that uses an onstage orchestra. For one thing, all the workings are out in the open. The interaction between performers and musicians is not only acknowledged, but also made central to the production.

I have directed fifteen musicals, and six of them—including *Tintypes, Once upon a Mattress, The Beggar's Opera*, and *Stop the World, I Want to Get Off*—featured the orchestra on stage in full view of the audience (not behind a scrim) and in costume.

When It's Right

I don't recommend this approach for every musical. As with any directorial choice, putting musicians on stage should not be an arbitrary one. It must work for you and for the show.

The concept works best with small-cast musicals, since the orchestra takes up space on the stage. However, space is not the only consideration. Even if you have a stage the size of Radio City Music Hall, it might be difficult to justify the presence of an onstage orchestra in the midst of *Oklahoma!* or *Annie*.

Among other considerations, the show in question must either invite a degree of stylization in which the orchestra can play a part (as in *Stop the World*), or allow you to include the musicians in the action realistically (as in the case of *Tintypes*, in which they performed in a band shell at the center of the stage).

Aside from the novelty aspect, putting the instrumentalists on stage helps erase the physical gap between audience and performers (a plus with an intimate show), and improves the balance of sound between orchestra and singers without having to resort to microphones and amplification. The setup also provides some variety in visual presentation. The theater company for which I direct most often presents its large-cast shows in traditional proscenium fashion with the orchestra in the pit. However, the pit also can be raised by hydraulic lift to become a forestage that extends through the proscenium. Using the forestage provides new set and lighting design possibilities, and places the performers nearer the audience. At the same time, the orchestra, forced out of the pit, adds an additional visual element to a small cast.

In the shows I have directed, the number of musicians has been small, from three to fifteen. In two cases (including *Stop the World*), the orchestra was directly on the stage floor. In *Tintypes*, it was in a "gazebo" on a six-inch platform. In *The Beggar's Opera*, the musicians sat on a large platform that was elevated six feet above the floor and fitted with railings for safety.

Making It Work

Once you decide to put orchestra members on stage, read through the script and score carefully to see where you can make the most of their presence. Look for opportunities for interaction between cast and instrumentalists.

In *Tintypes*, the orchestra members entered casually, singly or in pairs, chatting, then set up and tuned in full view of the audience—just as they might for a turn-of-the-century concert in the park (which was the whole idea). Two young women, who delivered props and costumes to the actors on stage, also were seen carrying those items across the stage before the show began and during intermission. They paused to talk to the musicians in the gazebo; one quietly relayed the stage manager's go-ahead to the conductor when the show was ready to begin.

In *Once upon a Mattress*, a group of court musicians was worked into such numbers as "An Opening for a Princess," "Happily Ever After," "The Spanish Panic," and even the princess's bedtime scene with the nightingale.

For *The Beggar's Opera* (which has more than fifty songs) we used a unit set of platforms of various sizes and heights, with the orchestra on one of its own. This put it within close range of the performers, which we used to comic advantage in several spots. For example, when the orchestra began the introduction to yet another in a series of plaintive arias by young Polly, her parents turned upstage to the conductor, shaking their fists at him.

An onstage orchestra will not only need integrating into the show, but also will affect how you stage the performances themselves. Intimate shows, with no big choruses to project over the orchestra, especially benefit from the performers' proximity to the audience. Singers don't have to force to be heard, which saves their voices—especially if they are singing in less-than-comfortable vocal ranges. Performances can be more subtle as well because the actor is closer to the audience.

Hearing and Seeing

The first time I rehearsed with the orchestra on stage, the sound not only overpowered the singers at times, but also had a muddy quality. I noted that the cyclorama had been rolled up to protect it during set construction, exposing the concrete-block wall behind it. As a result, the accompaniment was not only coming straight out to the house, but was also radiating backward, hitting the wall and bouncing off—producing a slightly out-of-phase echo that muddied the sound and occasionally covered the singers. Once the cyc was lowered, the sound quality improved dramatically. The problem need not have been a wall; any hard surface behind the orchestra could cause the same problem.

Logistically speaking, the greatest problem is that the actors can't see the conductor and vice versa. This means that everyone must be dead certain of entrances and tempos. Extra music rehearsal will be needed.

Some directors solve this problem by installing video monitors so the actors can see the conductor's downbeat. However, it's difficult to do this unobtrusively, and can become an unwelcome light source for the lighting designer to contend with. In all my shows, we have had a microphone placed near the front of the stage, and a black speaker (audio monitor) placed near the conductor. This allows him or her to stay in synch with the singers.

If rehearsing with an emphasis on tempos and entrances doesn't solve the problems, there are some simple tricks you can use. In one show, we added a bass part to the orchestration so that the cast would be able to feel the beat. In another, we replaced a bass-drum accompaniment with a snare drum because its higher frequency was more easily heard.

Songs demand cues between conductor and singer. When the singer faces the orchestra, the conductor can give the cue. When the singer faces away from the orchestra, the conductor must watch for the cue.

In *Tintypes,* a long spoken number has to be cued precisely to the underscoring. At one point, the orchestra vamps for a considerable time, waiting for the cue line, "Fear God!" However, in rehearsal, the cast was making so much noise that the conductor could not hear these words, so the orchestra kept vamping instead of moving on. As a solution, I had the actor raise his arm in a strong gesture on the words, "Fear God!," which was the visual cue the conductor needed.

A quite opposite problem occurred in *The Beggar's Opera,* in which we placed a microphone next to the harpsichord because the instrument was so far up stage and could not otherwise be heard. The amplification was subtle, so the eighteenth-century quality of the music was preserved.

The ultimate answer to sound-level problems is to mike the performers. Unfortunately, this is a complex art and, if done with too heavy a hand, sounds worse than no electronic help at all. Besides, my personal prejudice is for as "pure" a theatrical experience as possible. Amplified sound in the theater is too often forced, too loud, and doesn't reflect the performer's movement on the stage.

Suddenly They're Actors

Given the logistics of staging a production with an onstage orchestra, one might overlook the psychological considerations. In my experience, the pit orchestra is always somewhat removed from the rest of the cast and crew. By putting them on stage, this relationship changes dramatically. Actors and instrumentalists become better acquainted and general morale improves considerably. Many musicians also enjoy being able to see the whole show, instead of catching brief glimpses (if even that) from the confines of the pit.

At the same time, it should be said that some orchestra members may feel uncomfortable on stage, in full view of the audience, and behind the cast. Suddenly, they are actors and will need some help on stage presence. After all, in the pit they can do pretty much what they want, but on stage in view from the house, they must follow some rules: no white styrofoam cups (they reflect the light and/or are anachronistic); keep the area clean; don't look off stage or talk to each other unless directed to do so.

In the shows I directed, the musicians were fitted with costumes. In general, we pulled these from stock with minimal alteration, since they would not be seen up close in full light. In one show, the costumer created matching shirts and blouses. In two cases, the conductor needed a special costume designed. However, the orchestra won't need special makeup if they are never in full light and always at the back of the stage.

Avoid Distractions

Using lower light levels for the orchestra than for the performers is also the easiest way to focus attention on the stage action. Otherwise, look for ways to keep the orchestra placement from distracting unnecessarily.

I recall seeing a production of *Candide* staged in the manner of the 1974 Harold Prince production. In that concept, the theater is turned into a series of performing spaces, with the audience and actors vying for space. In this particular production, the orchestra was also divided and the conductor sat center, in a billowing white shirt that caught the lights so vividly that the audience's attention was constantly diverted. To avoid this problem in *Tintypes*, we put the conductor in a chair and kept his arm movements somewhat covered by one of the posts that supported the gazebo.

I prefer that the orchestra set up before the house is opened. They can make sure their music is organized, and place large instruments such as the drums, string bass, or piano. Those with smaller instruments (violin, flute, clarinet, and trumpet) can bring them on with them. Doing things this way presents a more organized picture to the audience, and makes it easier for the musicians to get into place quickly.

While all these elements will be new to most musicians, most are delighted to finally be seen doing what they do best—playing an instrument. Like actors, they will do what you want if they know it will make them look good.

Another View

Malcolm Bowes, a sound expert who has written a number of articles for *Stage Directions*, says that he has always thought it was an interesting concept to make the musicians part of the mise-en-scene. "After all," he says, "the Oriental theater has been doing it for centuries." However, he admits that his own reasons for going this route have had more to do with theatrical necessity than aesthetic adventure.

"Our pit at IUP [Indiana University of Pennsylvania] is extremely shallow and the sound coming up from it literally creates a sonic wall between the stage and the audience," he explains. Putting the orchestra on stage, behind the performers, removed the wall. "So it was really a practical decision," he adds. "That did lead to some interesting artistic decisions, however."

The big test came when the university mounted *Pal Joey* with the orchestra on stage. "Initially, they could be seen vaguely behind a scrim," Bowes says. "For the Chez Joey scenes [much of the show takes place in a tacky nightclub], we raised the scrim and they became the 'house' band—we eliminated the strings—and were dressed accordingly, depending on whether it was a 'rehearsal' or a 'perfor-mance.' In other words, we tried to integrate them as much as possi-ble with the book of the show. The band had a ball—a bunch of hams."

Bowes reports some acoustical problems that were solved by inte-grating the bandstand into the set design. "Indeed, by having the pit on stage, we saved ourselves a lot in construction costs. The band shell was the set," he explains, echoing my own experience with *Tintypes*.

Bowes calls the concept "an exciting one which, though it has its problems, also poses some wonderful artistic opportunities, assum-ing you are working with musicians who are willing and who under-stand the concept. I think it makes for an even more integrated kind of musical theater than most people realize is possible."

Final Thoughts

Whether or not you can benefit from an onstage orchestra will depend on the layout and acoustics of your theater. Experiment a bit. Before you do a full-scale book show, you might want to try an onstage orchestra for a revue or concert-style show. Try positioning the musicians in different parts of the stage; use electronic augmen-tation or monitoring only if absolutely needed.

Going with this concept can add excitement—visually, dramati-cally, and musically—to many shows. True, it requires new patterns of thinking in terms of design and direction, but the results can be well worth it.

"Take a Little One-Step, Two-Step"

24

It's a problem that crops up with almost every show: you have actors who can't sing and singers who can't act. What may be even more common, though, is having actors and singers who can't dance. Here's some advice on how to deal with that problem.

Choreography for Non-Dancers

One of the challenges in community or academic theater is putting on a musical with performers who have had little or no dance training. In some instances, actors are cast as much for their singing ability—or even their physical appropriateness for the part—as for their ability to move comfortably in time to music.

Choreographing non-dancers calls for patience, understanding, and a strong ability to communicate. It also calls for a different work method than that used with trained dancers. We asked a group of choreographers with experience in working with community, high school, and professional productions for their thoughts about this subject. We were not surprised to learn that they shared much common ground.

Motivating performers to do their best is essential, they all agreed. A key in this process is the choreographer's clearly stated role within the production team. "If the cast sees the staff as a team," says university teacher/choreographer Nancy Santamaria, "respectful of each other's creativity and position, the cast takes their cue and a working attitude of creativity and respect is developed. This structure can really bring a cast together, and even the most inexperienced actor can learn, grow, create, perform, and enjoy the process of theatrical production."

The place to begin this teamwork is at the beginning. The choreographer should have a vote in the audition process so that those chosen can at least handle the basics. In singing, you can give someone a lower note or mask their inadequacy in some other way. But a bad dancer sticks out like the proverbial sore thumb.

Communication Is Key

"Art is communication," says choreographer Jo Rowan, "so with the performers' health and self-respect in mind, I concentrate on what I'm trying to express and then, to quote two non-dancing geniuses, 'Form follows function' and 'Keep it simple, stupid.'

"The choreographer is responsible for making the process as rewarding as the performance," Rowan continues. "He should know not only how to dance, but also how to teach the basics of dance. As an example, knowing the essence of steps done in three-quarter time helps a performer master a movement and enjoy a feeling of accomplishment—for example, learning that 'balance' is a movement that steps away from center, while 'pas de bourree' is done closing the working leg under, and 'waltz turns' brush through the center of balance." Also, knowing that one has successfully learned a step called the Lindy may offer a greater reward than putting together a series of what might seem to be unrelated moves.

"A choreographer also has to trust that the performers will go beyond expectations," Santamaria adds. "They need to feel the responsibility of their own individual creativity in their contributions and the power that goes along with that. I have seen many good young actors emerge from the chorus motivated to learn more because of the initial freedom and encouragement given to them at the start."

Keep It Simple

Simplicity was the byword for most of the choreographers. "A choreographer can succeed in disguising the inadequacies of technique by choreographing movement patterns that contain the basics of dance steps, emphasizing dynamics and concentrating on the message that he wants to send to the audience," says Rowan. "Then, with simplicity in mind, rehearse and rehearse for cleanliness, because the choreography will only have dynamics and meaning if the audience can see and understand what I call the 'kinetic message.' You don't need great dancers to say something wonderful to the audience, but you must have sharp, clear movement."

Jennifer Medver agrees: "Simple but eye-catching choreography is the key. Intricate patterns and formations with lots of arm movement, as opposed to lower body movement, can be just as appealing to the eye of the audience, as well as to the morale of the performer."

Simplicity may mean that some musical numbers won't be danced at all. It is always important to question the justification for each inclusion of a danced number in a musical, for one can indeed "over-dance" a show. When this occurs, the audience may lose sight of the plot or the dancers may be taxed beyond their ability to perform. Sometimes it is better to stick with gesture and simple movement for most songs, while reserving the big guns for the numbers that need extra energy.

Keep in Character

A choreographer must understand the actor's process of developing a character, says Haila Strauss, director of The Special Dance Workshop for Actors in New York City. "If the actor's characterization is clear—emotionally and physically—the dance steps will just naturally flow, and the choreography will fall in place," she says.

Character-driven movement is the key, agrees Broadway choreographer A.C. Ciulla. "If the actor gets to dance or move through the character, it helps so much." Props also can help, because the actor can relate to them on a whole other level of characterization, Ciulla says. The Broadway cast of *Footloose*, for example, rehearsed a bar scene without their costume accessories. But when the actors were given boots and country-western hats, "all of a sudden they changed the way they carried themselves, and the personality came out through the movement," recalls Ciulla.

Once actors feel comfortable, their dance numbers require sustained emotion. Sometimes a move doesn't feel right anymore; it hurts or becomes boring after a while, says Ciulla, so he may change bits of the choreography. "It's important that you constantly love what you are doing. You can't fake that energy on stage," he told his *Footloose* cast.

For their part, performers should respect the art form of dance as an equal to acting and singing, says dance coach and choreographer Maria M. Torres. "It makes it easier to feel the dance, instead of just learning the steps." Torres says she adapts her choreography if an actor brings some other strength to the process. "The actor or performer may not be a great dancer," she says, "but surely has talent that can be translated."

She gets to know the actors on a personal level. "They have some story to tell, a piece of that person needs to be addressed and nurtured. When I develop choreography, I need to personalize it and relate it to the actor."

Ciulla spends time with his performers as well, learning as much as he can about them. Sometimes he discovers hidden abilities they didn't even realize they had, such as doing flips or spinning on their back. Even skills that don't have a formal, polished look—like gymnastics or skateboarding—can enhance dance routines.

Keep It Safe

Simplicity encourages safety as well. As dancer/choreographer Lyn Cramer points out, "In order to preserve the physical safety of actors and singers on stage in dance numbers, use innovative staging and dynamics to give energy and vitality to what must be simple, clean, basic steps for non-dancers."

She is seconded by colleague Nikki Singer, who believes that keeping non-dancers safe means "not overusing untrained muscles by creating dances that cause repetitive stress to a limb or body part."

"Safety is a strategic issue," says Santamaria, "because oftentimes you have cast members trying things like lifting partners, stage combat, or gymnastic stunts that they have never studied. First, you must examine the rehearsal surface. If the floor is concrete or tile on top of concrete, you have a dangerous situation. Floors should be hollow or raised or at best sprung wooden surfaces. But this sometimes means scheduling most of the major dance rehearsals on stage. You need to help the director understand how important this is to the safety of cast members, particularly young people whose bodies are still developing."

Rowan agrees. "To ensure safety, muscles that are unused or untrained must be warmed up. Therefore, a short, formal warmup is in order prior to all rehearsals. This should be followed by a 'marked run-through' of any choreography that has been learned."

Marking means that the performers move from place to place within the choreographed patterns, verbalizing what they are doing ("Left, left, left, pivot back, bend right . . ."), but avoiding leaps and lifts. As Rowan points out, "'Marking through' a routine before being asked to dance 'full out' allows the performers to refresh their memories while it warms the muscles that will be used."

Many safety problems can be solved before they appear. "This sounds almost too ridiculous to mention," says Santamaria, "but accidents do happen because of inappropriate attire. Also, cast members should not try stunts or combat without some working understanding of what is involved. Make this a firm policy: No experimentation, no horsing around. What's usually needed is a crash course on how to execute the move; how *not* to execute the move, and the consequences of doing so; and finally, how to 'spot' in order to help others practice. Spotters are a must. I teach the cast how to spot so they can practice with each other when I'm occupied elsewhere."

Work with What You've Got

"Making singers with limited dance ability look good on stage, without injury, lies in the ability of the choreographer to assess what they are able to do well," says Susan Webb. "Then, utilizing their strengths, create big but concise, simple movement. Once taught, the numbers should be rehearsed in a positive environment so that the performer feels comfortable and confident with the given movement."

Says Melanie Schultz, "If some performers have more ability than the rest, I feature them in solos or small groups. Blocking also adds interest to inventive choreography that is within the reach of performers. Clever blocking of simple steps also means that injuries are less likely to happen while the choreography retains its hold on the audience."

Sometimes the choreographer's vocabulary makes all the difference. "I have choreographed several shows for a light-opera company whose performers are singers, not dancers," says University of California Professor Harry Johnson. "When I work with them, I never use the word *dancing*. It scares a lot of people, especially men. Instead, I say we're going to do some exercises to loosen up, or that we're going to do some movement in this number. You can get people to do things they wouldn't do otherwise. They can learn better, too, because there's less pressure on them. They're not learning a dance, they're 'just' moving to the music."

One of Johnson's favorite dance routines came about strictly by accident. "I had planned a routine for a production of *H.M.S. Pinafore*," he recalls, "but in rehearsal I found that almost no one could do it. I tried to think of something new, but nothing was coming. I was frustrated; they were frustrated. I told everyone to sit down while I sorted things out. After a few minutes, I looked up and watched them do things as they sat. I noticed that off their feet they were much more at ease. Some were even doing the steps sitting down. That's when it hit me: we would do the number on the stage floor. They would do all the kicks and hand movements, but from a seated position. The audiences loved it. The critics loved it. I still get comments about it, years later."

Johnson recommends paying close attention to the performers and using not only their strengths, but also their ideas. "For example, you might play some music and have cast members make up a step or movement that fits the music," he suggests. "Have them do it in character. You'd be surprised what good stuff can come out of that. And again, because they helped create it, they do it with more confidence. It's a good morale-booster, too."

A special challenge is working with someone who has had dance training, but not in the style used in the current production. Santamaria recalls a production of *Anything Goes*, in which "one of the angels who accompany lead Reno Sweeney was a singer, actress, and ballerina. She has a great voice and is a good young actress to boot. But this was her first tap-dance experience. She worked endlessly to conquer the tap combinations in the title number. She was great in performance. Maybe all the beats weren't there, but I received more compliments about her dancing than any other chorus member. I think this was a matter of good casting. We knew she was better for the part, read well, sang well, showed herself to be committed and responsible. Her dance training, even if it was a different form, contributed to her ability."

All the choreographers stressed making the performers feel good about what they do well. This avoids many problems as you begin to shape the choreography during rehearsal.

Don't Lock Yourself In

The choreographers we talked with agreed that the choreographer must remain flexible. While it's important to preplan the choreography, they stressed that it's foolish to come in with a preplanned routine and expect it to be learned and performed exactly as you had it in mind.

"Sometimes as directors or choreographers we get locked in to something because we don't want to admit that we don't have everything solved from day one," says Johnson. "That works against the notion of theater as a creative process."

To avoid this trap, explain to the performers the role of experimentation in the initial rehearsal sessions. There may well be a need to change steps and positions that the dancers have learned already. No choreographer should be expected to set the routine in the first rehearsal and not to change it thereafter. First, this would rule out your using inspirational ideas for movements (such as Johnson's floor-bound routine) and ideas that come out of the rehearsals themselves. Second, you will find that some performers show unexpected ability in dance as they progress through rehearsal. You may want to go back and give them more to do. And, of course, others may not improve in their ability to do certain steps; you may need to revise to give them something else to do.

"I had blocked out most of the dances for one show ahead of time," recalls Johnson. "In rehearsal we worked real hard with lots of breaks for the cast to rest. I would go off stage and watch them do things during the break—new movement or variations on what we had done. I took the best things and put them in. They thought their stuff was silly and unimportant, but I used it throughout the show. I recommend this approach. People don't forget what they've created themselves."

Johnson, along with the others, points out that choreographing a chorus provides opportunity as well as challenge. Because of its size it encompasses many levels of dance ability. However, you also can use a wide range of activity, from a stationary tableau with its natural stance, to the held pose, to small movements such as a sway or change of weight from one foot to another. In many ways, a large group of people generates energy simply through their presence. By the same token, smaller, more controlled movements that may seem lacking in energy for a solo or duo may gain in strength when performed by a chorus—especially if the group is so large that it fills the stage.

The Voice of Experience

When you do assign specific movement, consider breaking the group into smaller units of three or four people. That is one of the tricks of the trade that Susan Wershing (former Rockette and founding publisher of *Stage Directions*) discovered in many years of working with community-theater groups.

"Put the best dancers in one group and place them in the center, with the other groups around the periphery swaying or doing simple steps. You get the effect of a unified pattern of movement, but you're not asking too much from those who aren't good on their feet. Or have the two or three trained dancers do the big steps while the others in the chorus stand in a semicircle behind, swaying or clapping."

Wershing also is a firm believer in props and effective costuming to help non-dancers. "People feel more confident if they don't have to worry about what to do with their hands. A prop—like a cane, parasol, or bouquet—can help a lot. It also draws audience attention upward, away from the feet. To create an effective stage picture, make sure they all carry the parasol or cane at the same angle."

Costuming to draw attention away from the feet is another trick Wershing has used, or designing sleeves that must be held away from the body in order to avoid the stiff-as-a-stick look.

A Sense of Self-Importance

Ultimately, working with non-dancers in a musical calls for all the patience and skill a choreographer can muster. However, you are not alone in this effort.

"Give each person [in a dance scene] a sense of importance," suggests Santamaria. "When they know the job they have to do and the importance of their individual work in telling the story, they will do anything to achieve that goal—even if it's endless hours of practice on a dance or staging that is difficult for them."

"Something to Dance About" | 25

It's bad enough if your actors and singers can't dance. But even if they can—how can you move them around if you're not a dancer? What kind of choreographic skills do you need? Inventiveness, for one.

How One Non-Choreographer Coped

STEPHEN PEITHMAN

Several years ago, I agreed to direct *Tintypes*, stepping in at the last minute to replace a director/choreographer who had been chosen precisely because the show would benefit from his dance expertise. While I have directed many musicals, and have created some basic stage movement in the process, I am not a choreographer.

Four of the five cast members were dancers, and three were also choreographers—a somewhat daunting situation, perhaps. As I thought about the show, the question came up: Should I allow the performers to choreograph their own numbers?

I asked this question of one of the performers, who responded, "I can choreograph other people, but I can't choreograph myself." Another said he could choreograph himself and his partner if I gave them the overall concept, while another was content to work on his own solo number only.

Given this, plus the need to get on with the rehearsals, I blocked the show, including the dance numbers, giving a strong sense of what each element was to accomplish. This allowed me, as director, to make sure every part of the show referred to my overall concept.

Within this framework, however, performers were free— and, as a matter of course, invited—to modify and improve what I had done. In some cases, the final choreography bore only the outline of what I had first blocked; in other cases, it was almost identical.

I surprised myself in my ability to come up with useable movement; my biggest liability was the lack of a repertory of dance styles and steps, and of a vocabulary to explain the precise steps I wanted. I often had to show or describe a step I had seen others do and then ask what it was called. Then a real dancer could demonstrate for the others. To provide the outline for what I wanted, I had to come up with some way to write down the kind of movement or effect I needed. Originally, I penciled in steps and blocking next to the lyrics in the script. Because I changed this so often as I worked before each rehearsal, the pages soon became full of indecipherable pencil marks and erasures.

My solution was to turn to my computer. In my word-processing program, I typed in all the lyrics in uppercase letters, leaving a space between each line. I then typed in blocking ideas directly below each line, only in lowercase letters. This allowed me to try things out in my head (and in my home), then redo the blocking as often as needed. I then printed out the results, put them in a three-ring binder, and took them to rehearsals. This gave me a clear view of what was going on; as we made changes in rehearsal, I penciled them in. If the changes became great, I edited the computer version and printed out new pages.

Here's an example of how this looked ("E," "T," "a," "C," and "S" refer to characters in the show):

IT'S FIFTY-FIFTY, IT'S FIFTY-FIFTY

Face out

NOT SIXTY-FORTY, NOR SEVENTY-THIRTY

E turns out R, then S turns out L

Outside shoulders should touch

I'VE FIGURED YOUR PERCENTAGE, HONEY, IT WON'T DO

Point to audience on "your"

YOU'VE BEEN CHEATING ME AND I'VE BEEN SQUARE WITH YOU

Thumb on fist to chest, then point out

I'M GETTING EVEN, IT'S EVEN-STEPHEN

Move down L

I'M WISE TO YOUR LIES CAUSE YOU'VE OPENED UP MY EYES

Stop: touch L hand to R knee on "wise"

Touch R hand to L knee on "lies"

Touch L hand to R shoulder on "open"

Touch R hand to L shoulder on "up"

Both hands to face on "eyes"

For a more complex dance, I used < > marks to indicate direction of movement or the direction a performer is facing:

KEEP UP SPEED, TAKE THE LEAD, THIS IS YOUR ONLY CHANCE

Kick-walk, rotating in circle; when done, woman should be facing away from center and be downstage of man

Start   Finish
E> <a   T> <C
<T C>   <E a>

I found this approach a useful tool. Perhaps others will as well.

26 | *Since You Asked*
Choreographing, Collaborating, Creating

Q: I've directed a few musicals before, but I'm a bit scared about this particular show I'm doing next. I don't have a choreographer this time, so I'm going to have to do that job myself. I have some idea of what to do, but I'm not trained in dance. Is there a book or video that can help me?

A: Yes, on both accounts. First, however, we have a few words of reassurance. Remember that "dance" is organized movement. It doesn't always need to be flashy. Indeed, choreography isn't always "dancing"—it may be walking, pointing, or head movement. Save the big guns for those places in the show where you can exploit the energy that dance supplies.

The best book on the subject is undoubtedly *Choreographing the Stage Musical*, by Margot Sunderland and Ken Pickering (ISBN 0-87830-030-9, Routledge). It's well written and includes lots of illustrations.

Also helpful is a videotape: *Step by Step: An Amateur's Video Guide to Choreography*, available from Pioneer Drama Service (see Chapter 37, "I Can See It"). This sixty-minute production is packed with helpful ideas and reassures by pointing out the similarity to blocking a scene. (Pioneer Drama Service; P.O. Box 4267, Englewood, CO 80155-4267; 800/333-7262; <www.pioneerdrama.com>)

Q: Do you have any tips on collaborating with choral music teachers or choral directors who know nothing about theater (but think they do!)?

A: The average choral director is used to a situation in which the singing (usually a concert) is an end in itself. But in musical theater, singing is a means to an end—the telling of a story and the illuminating of character. Indeed, singing is only one of several elements that contribute to the show's success—acting, costumes, sets, choreography, lighting, and so on.

A good vocal director must understand this. Certainly, in a musical, the role of the vocal director is important, but he or she must still work as a member of a team.

When working with collaborators, begin by stressing the importance of their contribution as it pertains to the total production effort. Make clear what you are trying to achieve and ask for help from your collaborators to make it happen. In the case of the vocal director, explain how you see the choral numbers integrating with your basic vision of the production. Then ask how he or she can help you reach that goal.

It's essential to schedule a meeting with all members of your creative team (directors and designers) early on. Again, explain your vision of the show and ask for ideas on how to achieve it. This makes clear that you intend to be in charge but are open to ideas from others.

There's another reason for one or more group sessions: by explaining your vision and delineating responsibilities, you have witnesses to what is expected from each person, and there's less of a chance that one of the collaborators will go his or her own way later on. The group meeting also underscores that this is indeed a team effort—that no one can change direction without causing problems for the others on the team. This makes it easier for you to rein in a team member without it seeming like a personal vendetta. You'll get better results working with collaborators when you treat them as collaborators.

Ultimately, of course, a director must have final say. But a good director knows when input from others can enrich his or her own vision of the production, and when those ideas can truly undermine it.

Q: What if you are going to put on a musical, but have trouble putting together a live orchestra for the run of the show? What would you do for a music source?

A: The answer depends on the musical, but many companies do fine with a piano, a percussionist, and a bass player. The problem comes mostly when you need a "big" sound, as in *Hello, Dolly!*. Some companies get around this by adding an electronic keyboard that can mimic trumpets, strings, and woodwinds. However, if your audience is used to hearing a full orchestra, even this may sound anemic. We would argue that it's better to choose shows that you can mount with the resources at your disposal, whether they be costumes, sets, or musicians.

Although it's true that accompaniment tapes are advertised in publisher's catalogues, the licensing agreement also will tell you that these tapes are to be used only for rehearsal purposes, and that it is a violation of the agreement to use recorded music in performance. That doesn't even address the headaches (and they are considerable) of integrating recorded music and live performers. Go with piano only, or piano, bass, and drums, if you can afford it.

PERFORMING THE MUSICAL
Tips for On Stage and Off

*L*ike the director, the musical-theater performer has many challenges not faced by those in nonmusical theater. There are the singing and dancing, of course. There also are observing musical cues, dialogue over underscoring, keeping an eye on the conductor, breath support, and projecting over the orchestra. It's a bit like being a juggler, keeping one's mind on several different things at once, while giving the impression of effortlessness.

In this section, we look at ways in which the actor becomes part of the collaborative effort that is a musical production. Performers also will find a great deal of useful information presented in earlier sections, including chapters on the elements of the musical ("Putting It Together," Chapter 2), and the comments on character transformation (Chapter 13).

27 | "I Hope I Get It"

Before you appear in a musical production, you have to get the role, of course. Each performer—as well as each director, naturally—has had different experiences during auditions. Each actor approaches each audition differently—some with trepidation, for instance, some with tremendous eagerness. That's why so many different people can offer so many varied tips on how to approach the audition and make it successful for you. In fact, occasionally the tips might seem contradictory to each other. That's because each tip has been formed by the specificity of particular experience and may or may not be applicable for you and your situation. But taken together, all the tips that follow point to one overriding admonition: Be prepared.

How to Make a Good Impression

NANCIANNE PFISTER

The actor was bemused. After his audition, he'd been invited to callbacks, where he was then asked to a second callback. When the casting was completed, he did not have a role. The director, while pleased with the actor's work, explained that she did not cast him as Major-General Stanley in *The Pirates of Penzance* because, she said, he was too tall.

You might wonder how much taller the actor had grown between the first audition and the second callback. But the truth is, most directors make casting choices based on the appearance of the entire show. If an actor looks out of place, the overall image for which the director is striving can suffer. As a performer, you have little control over the vision of the director.

But what about those things in an audition that you can control? Are you missing out on roles because you've neglected some detail that would show the director how effective you would be in this production? With only minutes to make an impression, the slightest sloppiness can result in your not being cast. Consider these twenty-five audition hints, drawn from our experience and from the advice of directors around the country.

Read the audition notice carefully so you know what will be expected of you. Will there be cold readings? Do you need to prepare a monologue? If so, how long should it be? Should it come from the script or from another source? Will you be asked to sing? To dance? To work with an animal?

Always find out if you must wear special clothing. Musicals usually call for heavy movement or dance, and you can't show your skills in a tight skirt or pants.

If you can, *get a script and read it.* Familiarize yourself with the material so you can understand the characters. Ask also if a score is available, so you can see in what keys the songs are written.

If you are asked to prepare something, prepare. One director told us she felt "insulted" when an actor auditioned for a musical with a song he had not prepared. He may have been under the mistaken impression that since he knew the director, he didn't have to impress her. He did impress her, however—negatively. Another director said he had asked all those auditioning to prepare a one-minute monologue. One person got up, rattled on for almost one minute about how she hadn't had time to prepare, then launched into a stop-and-start attempt at her monologue. "If she'd just gone ahead and done the monologue, I might have given her the benefit of the doubt," he said. "But after her long-winded excuses, I was more prepared to murder her than cast her."

Be on time. Better still, be early. In group auditions, key people usually will be introduced and there will be announcements about audition procedures, the method of notifying the cast, and the length of time from auditions to casting completion. You will want to know what's going to happen.

Turn off your electronic pager, cell phone, and wristwatch alarm. If the other part of your world can't function without you for a couple of hours, a director could wonder how it will survive a rehearsal and performance schedule.

Bring a pen. There will be forms to fill out. Pencil will smudge and is more difficult to read in a darkened theater. If your handwriting is less than clear, print. No one has time to decode.

List every phone number where you can be reached. It is amazing how often actors at an audition say they do not wish to divulge their home phone numbers. If you have concerns about your personal safety, get an answering machine and screen your calls. If it's not OK to be called at work, don't list your work number, and tell the casting people why. Also, tell of any plans to be away from home in the next few days. If you can't be found, you won't be cast.

If you're a newcomer to the company, bring a resumé. The degree of formality varies with each company, but no director will be insulted if handed a clean, thorough, well-prepared resumé. Bringing a resumé does not excuse you from completing the company's required audition form, even though much of the same information will be needed. Your resumé will go into the company files; the audition form is show-specific.

Bring a photograph, especially if you have never auditioned for this company. For a professional Actors Equity company, it is, of course, required. For smaller, nonprofessional theaters, a professional head shot would be great, but it is expensive; in some cases, a snapshot will do (ask ahead of time what is expected). The casting people need to remember what you look like. We know a company that takes Polaroid photos of each newcomer, but don't count on that. Do not submit a photograph in costume; that will make it more difficult for a director to imagine you in some other role.

Dress for the role you want. This doesn't mean be in costume; it means indicating by what you wear that you've done your homework, that you have some idea of the style of the show and the nature of your character. A woman auditioning for the role of the Mother Superior in *The Sound of Music* is unwise to do so in a frilly or low-cut dress. You may argue that the director should be auditioning you, not your wardrobe. You're right, but auditioning is not about being right. It's about making it as easy as possible for the director to envision you in the part you want.

Prepare! That seems so obvious as to be silly to mention it, but many people rely on past performances or experience with directors. These actors develop an attitude: "They've seen me work; I don't have to impress them." Yes, you do. A director may have seen you in the last show, but this is the next show. Instead of resting on your laurels, you should feel challenged to be twice as creative in your audition.

Be creative. The too-tall actor mentioned previously once had to audition for a director who was a long-time friend. They had directed each other and played opposite each other many times. Rather than think he need not bother to prepare, the actor looked for a way to have the director remember his doing something special. He sang his audition song the way four different characters in the upcoming show might sing it. He did not sing the song four times, but instead changed character throughout the song. To help his audience keep track of the roles, he used a 3 × 5 card with each character's name on it. As he changed characters, he displayed the card. This bit of nonsense resulted in a release of tension for the other auditioners, a smile from the director, and a role for the singer.

If you are asked to prepare a song or monologue, *be brief.* Too often, actors think they are choosing something for a one-man show or concert. But it's not a concert, it's an audition. Extended arias or songs with multiple verses should be left behind or shortened. In monologues, give yourself just enough time to warm up, then show off your abilities in a few bold strokes. The director will thank you for it.

Prepare a song in the same style as the show, but not from the same show unless specifically requested to do so. (Many directors prefer that you not sing something from the show to be cast until callbacks.) No matter how well you sing that country-western number, it won't show the directors that you can handle a Gilbert and Sullivan patter song.

Talk with the accompanist about your song. Do you want the second ending? Do you want the high note? (Thinking of singing a capella? Don't, unless there is no other option.) As professional musician David Pogue points out, "The pianist can make or break you; treat that pianist accordingly. Be friendly and appreciative. Briefly discuss your music. Indicate the tempo you prefer during a quiet, pre-performance meeting; one good way is to softly sing the first line to the pianist. Come prepared with readable, easy-to-use music whose pages have been taped together. You wouldn't believe the crumbling, disordered music pianists are handed—sometimes the music doesn't include a piano part at all."

When your name is called, *step into the audition space with energy and confidence.* Pause for a few seconds, then say, " Hello. My name is . . . ," then pause again. Since you've just been called by name, why would you do this? It's a way of saying that you are ready and the casting people should pay attention. Don't say, "I'm . . . " The extra four syllables give the casting crew time to focus on you, to look up from a form they are reading, or to finish a comment they are writing. Once you have commanded attention, announce your monologue or song, briefly supplying any background that you find necessary to set a mood. If you have edited your selection, now's the time to say so.

Whether you speak or sing, *project with the same energy you will use in performance.* If you cannot be heard, what's the point?

Whether you speak or sing, *enunciate with the same clarity you will use in performance.* If you cannot be understood, what's the point?

Whether you speak or sing, *use the language of the show being cast.* You may be the finest Figaro since Caruso, but if you sing his song, how will the directors judge your diction as Nicely-Nicely Johnson?

Play to the casting team. If auditions are open for all to watch, you'll have an appreciative and supportive audience, but your fate is not in their hands. Don't ignore them, but address most of your attention to the director, musical director, choreographer, producer, and anyone else who will have a say in casting. Just don't stare at them. Many directors find a direct gaze disconcerting.

When you've finished your song or monologue, stay where you are, waiting for any further requests or instructions. When the director says, "Thank you," return the courtesy and leave the audition space. Remember to thank the accompanist.

Be flexible. You've read a scene with another actor. Now the director says, "Read it as if you hated each other," or "Read it as if you shared a deep sorrow,' or "Read it as if you've just won the lottery." Give it your best shot, no matter how far out of character you feel. No one expects a polished performance; the director wants to know that you can accept direction and will take risks. If the musical director asks you to vocalize to your lowest note, do so without comment or excuse. (At one audition, the director asked a group of people reading a scene to be "silly as you can be." No one did so. If just one had taken the lead, the rest might have followed. Or if the rest didn't follow, at least the one actor who did as directed would have impressed the director.)

If auditions are open, stay and be part of an audience for the other performers, as they were for you. Some directors like to add theater games or exercises to an audition, so don't leave until you are certain you will no longer be needed.

If auditions run two nights or more, find out if you can come back and read or sing again. Some directors don't mind, others do. Don't ask to sing again unless you really think you can do better—if you do the same or worse, you're no better off.

Someone has compared auditions with the worst kind of job interview. You may never be totally at ease, but you can lessen the stress by paying attention to details. Being in control of your audition means you're more likely to be cast—no matter how tall you are.

(For more tips and advice, see *The Stage Directions Guide to Auditions.*)

"I'm the Greatest Star" | 28

You've gotten the part; now what do you do with it? How do you turn a great role into a great musical performance? Here are some ideas on getting to where you want to be.

Secrets to a Great Performance

A s we noted previously, the most common mistake of performers (and directors) is to view a musical merely as a play with music. That's not the case. If it were, you could remove the music and still perform what was left with little or no problem.

Strip *My Fair Lady* of its songs, and you don't wind up with *Pygmalion*—you end up with a story line, but no character development. Without "Why Can't the English?," we can't appreciate Henry Higgins's very real sense of humor. Without "An Ordinary Man," we wouldn't understand the internal (although flawed) logic of his behavior. "Wouldn't It Be Lovely?" expresses Eliza's dreamy side that we get almost nowhere else. Likewise, "I Could Have Danced All Night" foretells her developing feelings for Higgins. "Just You Wait" expresses her declaration of independence from the professor, just as his "I've Grown Accustomed to Her Face" expresses his own declaration of dependence on Eliza.

Or take a show as traditional in format as *Hello, Dolly!*. The opening number, "Call on Dolly," sets up Dolly as a person who sticks her nose into everybody's business. But it's clear from the song that everybody loves her because of it, not in spite of it. When Cornelius and Barnaby sing "Put on Your Sunday Clothes," it is more than a big number—it's an explosion of emotions that have been bottled up by their repressive existence in Yonkers. And when Dolly sings "Before the Parade Passes By," she is declaring her decision to grab the happiness that she deserves.

Actors in nonmusical productions often are asked to work on motivation, on the character's objective. It's common to

115

ask, "What does my character want in this scene, in this speech?" The same question—and others—must be asked of each song:

What is the one thing the singer wants that is expressed (or gained) through the song?

Why is this song sung at this place and time, and by this person?

Why does he or she sing it, rather than speak it?

Does the song develop or illustrate character? If so, what and how?

Does the song advance the plot or is it a charm song, simply there to entertain?

Is the song sung to someone else or does it represent the character's inner thoughts?

What happens just before the musical number and what happens just after? How is the show (or character) different after the song is performed?

What is the single most important thing the audience needs to understand when the song is finished? And how can the performer make that clear?

Let's look at how answering these questions can help you create a more powerful performance.

Some wit remarked that *Oklahoma!* is about whether or not Laurey will go to the box social with Curley. But that's only partly true. The real question is whether Laurey and Curly can get past their own pride and admit that they love each other. However, both are immature and more than a bit stubborn. It will take something big to shake up their world and force them to grow up.

The play, *Green Grow the Lilacs*, on which *Oklahoma!* is based, provides the starting point, a character named Jeeter. But Jeeter is a bit two-dimensional as a villain, so librettist Oscar Hammerstein transforms Jeeter into the deeply troubled Jud Fry. He becomes the driving force behind the transformation of Laurey and Curley. And that is why Jud's song, "Lonely Room," is so dark and menacing in comparison with the general sunniness of the rest of the show—particularly after Jud has been the butt of Curly's jokes in "Pore Jud is Daid." Because Jud is not a buffoon. He may not be quick-witted, but he is a menace.

In "Lonely Room," Jud lashes out at Curly ("I'm better'n that smart aleck cowhand who thinks he is better'n me!") and imagines that

Laurey ("the girl that I want") is his, with her "long, yeller hair" falling across his face, "jist like the rain in a storm!" But then his daydream ends, and he sees that his desires are "a pack o' lies" and he is left to lie "awake in a lonely room."

His final words are chilling, foretelling what will happen in Act II. He refuses to live in a dream world: "I ain't gonna leave her alone!/ Goin' outside,/Git myself a bride,/Git me a woman to call my own!"

When performed properly by a fine singing actor, "Lonely Room" should raise the hair on the back of your neck. Jud's threat is then underscored by the events in Laurey's dream ballet, setting up the dramatic confrontation that leads to Jud's death in Act II. Before "Lonely Room," Jud is merely a shadow. After it, he is a palpable presence, even when he's not on stage.

To take a less dramatic example, consider "On the Street Where You Live" in the second act of *My Fair Lady*. Why is this song here? It's a good song—it even became a top-ten hit. But it should not be an excuse to stop the action and serenade the audience.

It's sung by Freddy Eynsford-Hill, who has met Eliza at the race-track and is now totally smitten with her. That fact is made abundantly clear by his song, full of unabashed romanticism explicitly absent from any other song in the show. It's a song of overstatement from start to finish, with the kind of words that only someone head over heels in love would utter.

At one level, this indicates the transformation of Eliza Dolittle into someone who could captivate someone as high-born as Freddy. But it's clear from the words of the song that Freddy is no match for Eliza in temperament—or native intelligence. She is not a head over heels kind of woman, which she makes clear later when she sings to him, "Words, words, words, I'm so sick of words!" For it isn't words that Eliza needs, but respect from someone who will treat her as an equal. Freddy wants to put her on a pedestal.

That's why "On the Street Where You Live" suffers if performed as a charm song, as a mere entertainment, or to cover a set change. For it is essentially a character song. We need to feel Freddy's giddiness, not watch a stuffed shirt sing an aria. He sings because there is no other way he can express his emotions.

So, if you're cast as Freddy, how will you play the moment? The same can be asked of "Without You" and "I've Grown Accustomed to Her Face." "Without You" is a wonderful song, a strong statement. It's even funny, and at Higgins's expense (for once). But in Act I, Eliza also made a strong statement about Higgins, and it also was funny and at his expense—"Just You Wait." What's different here? Quite a lot, actually. "Just You Wait" was an angry war cry, but Higgins was nowhere around. Eliza was afraid of him then, but not anymore. Now she's got the upper hand, and she tells him exactly what she thinks of him. "Just You Wait" is a childish threat. "Without You" is a witty rapier thrust. The two songs, therefore, must be played very differently.

Higgins's evolution in the show is quite the opposite of Eliza's. He has spent most of the show making it quite clear that he is somehow independent of all other humans, that he is self-sufficient, a law unto himself. Then, in "I've Grown Accustomed to Her Face," he grows introspective for the first time. Of course he blusters through the process ("I shall never take her back, if she were crawling on her knees"), but in this song he also becomes human. And that is a transformation that is essential if we are to feel comfortable with Eliza's return at the end.

Most actors with any experience or training will recognize this sort of scene analysis. It's common practice in most schools and training programs. Strangely, however, many actors and directors don't use it in musical theater—perhaps because they have the mistaken notion that a song is just a song.

That's understandable in light of the history of musical theater. In most shows written before *Oklahoma!,* songs are essentially charm or comic songs, and dialogue takes the burden of plot development.

Anything Goes is a good example of this older style. The original production begins with the song "I Get a Kick out of You," but there's no context for it. We don't know why Reno is singing this particular song at this particular point. (The 1962 edition, most often performed today, begins with "Bon Voyage" to set the scene, then launches into "You're the Top.") And, as entertaining as they may be, "Anything Goes" and "Blow, Gabriel, Blow" have no bearing on the plot; they are there strictly to entertain. "You're the Top" does help us understand the deep friendship between Reno and Billy, just as "All Through the Night" makes clear Billy's attraction to Hope Harcourt. But the songs aren't particularly specific to their characters or situation. They could have been written for any Cole Porter show of the 1930s.

What later musicals did was to tie the song more closely to the book. Songs tend to flow naturally out of the situation and characters. Thus, if a song is treated as only that—a song—it may lose its emotional weight.

It's true that there are songs that are meant to have no deep emotional weight: examples include "A Bushel and a Peck" and "Take Back Your Mink" from *Guys and Dolls*, or any of the nightclub numbers in *Pal Joey*, or "The Lonely Goatherd" in *The Sound of Music*. We learn a lot about Adelaide and Joey's environment from their songs, and "The Lonely Goatherd" could be said to underscore the love between Maria and the von Trapp children. They are essential to the fabric of their show and deserve to be done well, but they provide no depths to plumb.

In the end, it's a matter of understanding and balance. By asking yourself the questions at the beginning of this chapter, you can determine the reason for the song and the reason for the character to sing it. You then can balance that understanding with the equally important task of performing the number in a way that is both musically and dramatically satisfying.

You'll find a valuable resource in Fred Silver's book, *Auditioning for the Musical Theatre* (ISBN 0-14010-499-2, Penguin), which touches on a number of these elements in his chapters "How to Act a Song" and "How to Play a Comedy Song."

29

"If They Could See Me Now"

How's Your "Lighting Sense"?

"Comfortable" lighting to an actor is in fact "rather in the nature of a controlled discomfort," writes Francis Reid in *The Stage Lighting Handbook*. Indeed, stage lighting is often glaring, hot, and—to many actors—faintly mysterious.

Sensitive musical theater performers feel the light, so they always know just how visible they are at any given moment. Sadly, many actors do not bother to learn how stage lighting works, or even the simple technique of judging their light.

Good lighting is essential to any portrayal of character. After all, if the audience can't see you, they're missing a lot. And in the musical, the use of stage lighting is often more complex than in nonmusical productions, making the challenge even greater. Here's a simple training program for any actor uncertain of his or her "lighting sense."

You'll need the help of your lighting director or light-board operator to run lights while you are alone on stage. Better yet, develop a mini-workshop of your fellow performers who feel the need for the same training. Just be sure to give yourself enough time to become confident in your ability to judge your light.

The first essential is to know when your face is illuminated. You probably have seen many actors overshoot their light, to end up in half-darkness, robbing their performance of impact. With the stage dark except for one instrument trained near the center, slowly walk into the light from the upstage side. Look down as you walk and you'll see that your feet hit the light long before your head.

As you move forward, more and more of your body is illuminated; as you move downstage and out of the light, your face is the last thing to be seen. In other words, when you move into a beam of light, you will need to aim for a stopping place somewhere between the center of the beam and its downstage edge.

A second essential is knowing when you are in the center of the light beam. This is called the *hot spot*, and with a little practice any actor can find it quickly. Again, ask for a single light on an otherwise dark stage. Of the two basic types of lights, the Fresnel and the ellipsoidal, the Fresnel hot spot is more obvious. Step into the light; if it is very bright, ask the light-board operator to bring it down to a comfortable level. Look straight at the light beam while moving your head left and right. You should find a point where the light seems to dim slightly, which means you have moved out of the hot spot. When you step forward or backward out of the center of the beam, you should notice the same dimming effect. (If you are in doubt, ask the lighting person to watch and tell you when he or she sees you move in or out of the hot spot. It may take several tries for you to sense accurately when your face is fully illuminated.)

A final safety note: A blackout after a brightly lighted stage (typical of most musicals) may cause you to have a temporary case of night blindness. If you must make a quick exit, you could trip over set pieces or even a fellow actor. One answer may be to request a safety light—such as a red bulb—directly off stage and in a clear pathway, to guide you off. Some actors close their eyes a moment or two before the blackout; this gives them a chance to adjust before the lights go out. If you can't close your eyes, look away from the glare of the hot spot just before the blackout. (Just be sure to tell your director what you're doing and why.)

30 | *"That Certain Feeling"*

When you're in a musical and you come down with a cold or flu, you may have no option other than to go on with the show. Most community theaters don't employ understudies, and without you the show might have to be postponed or closed.

Going on Sick (and Staying Well)

How does the performer get through the performance(s)? And how can the other performers protect themselves from contracting the same illness? Although a performer reacts to a cold or flu like any other human being, not all common treatments are advisable or even helpful. Current medical wisdom has these suggestions to help you through the rough spots.

Aches and Fever

Research indicates that fever is one of the body's ways of fighting infection. According to the Mayo Clinic, taking aspirin or acetaminophen will usually reduce a fever in adults. However, a temperature of 101 degrees that persists for longer than three days or a temperature of 103 degrees or more requires immediate medical attention.

Stuffy or Runny Nose

Avoid over-the-counter cold remedies with antihistamines such as diphenhydramine and chlorpheniramine. These may help dry up nasal secretions, but they can also dry your throat, leading to hoarseness. Antihistimines also can influence brain function, causing not only drowsiness, but also problems in remembering lines and cues or executing precision stage movement. If you suffer from nasal congestion, it's best to only take a decongestant-only product, such as pseudoephedrine, although these drugs have their own side effects in some people (such as irregular or slow heartbeat, shortness of breath, jitters).

As always, it's wise to check with your own physician to find out if you have special sensitivities to any nonprescription drugs. Or check the Mayo Clinic website, <www.mayohealth.org>, for information on various over-the-counter medications.

If you must use an antihistamine, some are more likely to cause dryness of the mouth than others (astemizole and terfenadine, for example, commonly produce this effect). For temporary relief of mouth dryness, when off stage use sugarless candy or gum, melt bits of ice in your mouth, or use a saliva substitute.

Avoid using most nasal sprays or drops. While these will relieve a runny nose and nasal congestion, their use may be followed by an increase in nasal congestion (called *rebound*), particularly when you use them over an extended period, such as the run of a show. Also, their effectiveness decreases with repeated use. The one exception is saline nasal spray; this is the best choice for the performer because it can be used as often as needed with no rebound effect.

Sore Throats and Coughs

This is of primary concern for the singer. Each time you cough, your airways are compressed. A harsh or forceful cough can irritate the lining (membranes) of your airways. Repeated coughing can lead to inflamed membranes, helping to perpetuate your cough—and damage your voice.

To ease the cough cycle, doctors recommend that you try these simple approaches:

Drink extra liquids. Sometimes secretions in your lungs become thick and sticky, making them difficult to remove by coughing. A cough that doesn't bring up mucus is nonproductive (dry). Drinking plenty of liquids, especially water, helps thin and loosen mucus to make your cough more productive. By bringing up mucus, a productive cough helps clear your airways of irritants. Beverages such as juices and hot tea can also soothe and lubricate your throat.

Breathe moist air. Taking a shower or using a humidifier or vaporizer also helps loosen mucus. Small portable models are available, allowing you to bathe just your nose and mouth in warm moist air.

Soothe your throat. Sucking on hard candy or cough drops, or drinking tea sweetened with honey, may help prevent coughing if your throat is dry or sore.

Try not to cough. Frequent dry coughing can worsen irritated airways. Try to cough as seldom and gently as possible. Taking frequent sips of liquids may help stifle the cough cycle. Harsh clearing of the throat also can irritate your vocal chords. As part of simple self-care for your cough, you can take an over-the-counter cough medicine. These medicines work to make your cough more productive or to quiet a disruptive cough. However, some are better suited than others for the performing artist.

- Expectorants: The name *expectorant* comes from the verb *expectorate*, meaning "to spit." These cough medicines contain guaifenesin, an ingredient that works to loosen mucus in your airways. As a result, expectorants can help clear your airways of irritants. Taking an expectorant-cough medicine, drinking plenty of water, and breathing moist air offers maximum loosening of mucus.

- Suppressants: To temporarily reduce the frequency of your cough, you can take a cough suppressant. These medications, also called *antitussives* (from the Latin word for cough), act directly on the cough center in your brain. Some prescription antitussives contain a narcotic such as codeine—not a good idea for anyone who must stay alert. Non-narcotic antitussives, such as dextromethorphan and diphenhydramine, are available in nonprescription cough medicines. These ingredients help relieve coughing without the risk of side effects associated with narcotics. If your cough brings up mucus, it's best not to suppress it. But if your cough is frequent and produces small amounts of mucus, the Mayo Clinic suggests you consider using a combination medicine containing both an expectorant and a suppressant.

- Expectorants plus suppressants: Some cough medicines contain an expectorant plus a cough suppressant. The expectorant helps loosen mucus while the cough suppressant reduces the frequency of your cough. In combination, these ingredients can make your cough more productive while making you more comfortable.

Rest

The pressures of preparing for performance and the performance itself are draining. You can't do much about reducing energy demands on stage, but you can take time for a nap or at least a lie-down before you go to the theater.

If possible, do your makeup at home, where you are less pressured. At the theater, make sure you have some place to sit comfortably when not on stage. Above all, avoid short-term remedies that may make for long-term problems.

Danger Signals

Remember that some serious diseases can mimic a cold. Measles and chicken pox have similar symptoms, but also produce a rash. Strep throat usually begins with a cold, but is accompanied by a sore throat, high fever, and severe chills. If you exhibit any of these additional symptoms, see a doctor immediately, particularly if a fever lasts for more than a few days or soars abnormally high.

Protecting Yourself

Traditionally, we've thought of colds as being spread when people sneeze, spraying germs into the air. However, recent studies show that colds and flu are most often transmitted by people touching their nose or mouth, and then touching surfaces that others may touch as well. So just being in the same cast with someone who's down with a cold doesn't mean that you will also come down with it.

You can protect yourself to some degree by washing your hands frequently— particularly after touching the infected person or something that person has handled, such as a prop or door handle. "Nothing beats diligent handwashing with soap and water when it comes to fighting bacteria," states Frank R. Cockerill, M.D., a microbiologist and infectious-disease expert at the Mayo Clinic. "Virtually all soaps have an 'antibacterial effect,'" he adds. "Soaps—antibacterial or not—help eliminate germs both by 'washing them away' and by disrupting the cell walls of bacteria, making it difficult for them to multiply."

Cockerill cautions that while antibacterial soaps may claim to keep hands "cleaner" longer with the addition of an antibacterial compound, the scientific evidence to suggest just how much protection is offered, or for how long, is lacking.

Using a hand-sanitizing liquid is another precaution, and perhaps easier than continually washing your hands backstage because there's no water needed. A small bottle will fit easily into a makeup kit.

(Suffice it to say, the sick person should not share makeup with any-one else.)

Finally, get plenty of rest. Taking on a role in a musical while you're also holding down a job, caring for a family, or going to school can take its toll. Pay attention to your body and avoid getting over-tired, which can lower your resistance to disease.

SETS, LIGHTING, AND SOUND

Dealing with Technical Challenges

*F*or the most part, musical theater works with the same technical issues as nonmusical theater. However, the special needs of the singer, dancer, and orchestra do create some additional challenges. In this section, we take a look at some of the ones most likely to be of concern.

"One"
The Advantages of the Unit Set

STEPHEN PEITHMAN

M any musicals create challenges for set changes, and for set design in general. Many originally were produced in large Broadway houses, where complex sets could be accommodated, and where machinery could do the work of changing sets. The result is that it's common for musicals to have many scene changes throughout, whether it is a large show such as *The Music Man,* or the more intimate *A Little Night Music.*

One way to get around the problem is with the use of a unit set. Here, there is essentially one large stationary set, divided into multiple playing areas. Ideally, as David Welker points out in his book *Stagecraft* (Allyn & Bacon), "the major scenic structure is relatively neutral and unobtrusive, given character by the addition of smaller but more noticeable units, which suggest the different locales."

The individual parts of the unit may be dressed simply with furniture or sketchy architectural elements to indicate an interior or exterior setting, and the shift from place to place is handled by bringing up the lighting on one area while dimming it on another. This not only cuts or eliminates set shifts, but may be ideal where there are unusual scenic demands or where theater space is inadequate.

Welker mentions the use of a unit set in *The Threepenny Opera*, whose action takes place in a London street, a clothing store, a barn, a brothel, and Newgate prison—the latter including the outside of a cell, the scaffold, and gallows.

Coincidentally, I used the same approach when directing *Threepenny*'s predecessor, *The Beggar's Opera*. My set designer fell ill at the last moment, and I was forced to design my own set. I decided to use three playing areas: the forestage, downstage, and center stage.

The center stage was a two-level platform, with a chamber orchestra situated on the taller, stage-left level. (See "The Music That Makes Me Dance," Chapter 23). We used only a few props and set pieces, gobos (lighting patterns), and sound effects to suggest locales. I also cast a young woman to come out and change a sort of vaudeville billboard that explained the setting. It worked very well.

So well that, three years later, I used a somewhat more complex unit set for a production of *A Little Night Music*. The musical is based on a film, and has a film-like way of changing locale. The original Broadway show got around this with marvelous sliding panels designed by Boris Aronson. Our theater (and budget) couldn't handle this particular solution, so my set designer, Ed Nordstrom, came up with a simple, elegant solution—a unit set providing a stage floor-level playing area downstage center, surrounded on the back and sides with platforms of different levels, in an inverted "U" shape.

There was one shift between acts, when the platform that had been Desiree's rented rooms in Act I was modified to be the front of the Armfeldt mansion in Act II. The rest of the platforms were dressed differently, using furniture and props—except for Mme. Armfeldt's parlor, which was the same in both acts. We also used a simple wagon for another playing space and a collapsible theater box for Act I. It was a simple set and yet highly attractive. It really helped add to the flow and ambiance of the show.

When I did the show again, ten years later, with a different designer, I asked for a unit set again. The look was different, but the show continued to benefit from the smooth flow from being able to move from scene to scene with just simple lighting changes.

32 | "Soft Lights and Sweet Music"

Keeping the Conductor in View

MIKE BROMBERG

*I*n musical theater, particularly opera, the cast must be able to see the conductor clearly. However, in a standard proscenium-stage/orchestra-pit arrangement, an unlit conductor against an unlit audience can be hard to make out when cast members are staring into bright frontlighting.

In my work with a Gilbert and Sullivan company, we usually try to provide some light on the conductor's face and arms from a steep frontlight. (Because the conductor faces upstage, it looks like a backlight on the plot.) A 100–150-watt three-inch Fresnel ("inky") on an overhead pipe does a good job, though a standard 500-watt six-inch Fresnel will do if you keep it dim to avoid blasting the audience's eyes.

But such a setup wasn't enough for our production of *The Gondoliers.* Here, our performance space was very wide and shallow, with the orchestra at stage left. The singers could see the conductor only by looking sharply to their left, and that was often precluded by the blocking. To make matters worse, the long distance between orchestra and stage created sound delays that sometimes caused the leads and chorus to get out of synch with the instrumentalists. Although this was not exactly a lighting problem, it was a visibility problem.

We came up with the innovative solution of casting the shadow of the conductor's arm on the wall behind the audience where the singers could see it. A 6 × 1-inch ERS ("Leko," although any long-throw ellipsoidal would do) on a floor stand was fitted with a "top hat" and a soft amber gel (Roscolux 17) and aimed upward to cast the shadow. The shutters were carefully arranged to keep light out of the eyes of both conductor and audience.

While the conductor couldn't see the shadow behind him, he could see the light on his arm, so he knew when the "message" was getting through. Result: a high-quality performance, no musical train wrecks, and a much-relieved cast.

33 | "The Music of Sound"

Where to Put the Speakers

MALCOLM BOWES

S ome years ago, while watching Angela Lansbury and Len Cariou dispose of a number of London citizens in *Sweeney Todd* in New York, I had an odd experience. Len and Angela were singing "A Little Priest" downstage center, but their voices seemed to be coming from somewhere to the right of the stage.

In fact, they were. For whatever reason, the sound-reinforcement speakers had been positioned on either side of the theater's large proscenium. As a result, my first instinct was to think the actors were lip-synching. I knew they weren't, of course, but the displacement of the sound was—to put it mildly—disconcerting.

Sound Should Come from the Stage

There is considerable debate about speaker placement. Optimally, you want the sound—music, effects, or vocal reinforcement—to come from the stage, or at least appear to do so. However, onstage speakers are not practical in most cases. For one thing, unless you really want to see them, they need to be masked; if you try to minimize them by positioning them upstage, you inevitably reduce their efficiency. If they are being used for voice reinforcement, placing them upstage increases the likelihood of feedback.

Some proscenium theaters have their own built-in systems. However, the equipment may or may not be suitable (it usually is not), and you also do not have much flexibility as to speaker selection and direction. Most theaters, however, have no permanent systems, so the issue of placement—permanent or temporary—can and must be addressed.

Since the goal is to position speakers so that the sound appears to come from the stage, your sound designer has really only two choices. As we'll see, the first is better than the second.

From on High

Ideally, speakers should be mounted in clusters, centered above the proscenium arch. Placing the speakers too far apart diminishes their effectiveness, since they begin to work against, and cancel out, each other. The speakers also need to be focused, so that the entire house is covered uniformly. The size and type of speakers used will depend on the size and overall acoustic quality of the theater.

This solution is best because the position is as close to the stage as possible without actually being on stage. Moreover, the human ear is far more sensitive to the direction of sound horizontally than vertically, so with proper equipment selection and positioning, the sound (at least for the majority of the audience) will appear to come from center stage. However, people sitting in the first few rows of the orchestra may have difficulty hearing the sound from the speakers. That might not be a problem if they are able to hear the actors or music directly, without reinforcement; otherwise consider adding directional speakers to the sides of the arch, focused on the front rows. These side speakers should be mounted on or near the top of the arch.

Since a cluster of speakers above the arch can be an eyesore, you may want to consider masking or camouflaging them. Black scrim works as well as anything.

Taking Sides

If you cannot mount the speakers atop the arch, you can use the sides of the stage. As you might expect, you run the risk of displacing the sound, especially for those sitting to the sides of the house—not to mention creating a sonic "hole" center stage, where you want the sound to come from. However, with careful selection, placement, and focusing, you can come up with a satisfactory solution.

Depending on the size of the auditorium, three or four speakers (sometimes more) should be used on both sides. Mount them vertically, but not piggyback. Most theaters that use this method prefer to use column speakers for their superior directionality. Mount the speakers on or near the top two thirds of the arch. If mounted too low they will lose their effectiveness.

For example, if you mount three speakers vertically on each side of the arch, each speaker should be directed toward a particular part of the seating area: the top speaker toward the rear, the middle speaker toward the center, the bottom speaker down front. Some more sophisticated setups allow for individual volume and equalization controls, which allow for more uniform sound throughout the auditorium. This can make a significant improvement, because different sound frequencies have different dispersal patterns.

Don't crisscross the speakers. Those on stage right should be used for house left, those on stage left for house right. The sound should overlap slightly in the center, not unlike lighting a basic acting area.

While not as effective as a cluster of speakers above the proscenium arch, this setup can give fairly good results, particularly for vocal reinforcement. Masking is more difficult in this position, however, since the speakers are in the audience's line of vision.

The Balcony Problem

Whichever method you use, if your theater is very large with a balcony, and the area under the balcony is unusually deep (fifteen rows or more), you have an additional problem. Underneath the balcony overhang the sound from the proscenium speakers is obscured. Some theaters use small "pilot" speakers mounted under the balcony to ease the problem. To ensure uniformity of sound, the signal going to these speakers is processed with a slight time delay, usually about 20 milliseconds (the standard used in Dolby Surround systems in movie theaters).

Other Considerations

There are all sorts of wall and ceiling rack-mounts you can purchase that not only ensure a firm, safe mounting, but also allow for proper positioning and focusing. Be sure that the wall or ceiling above and around the arch can accommodate the weight of the equipment. Be sure to aim the speakers toward the seating, not the walls, and dress the speaker cable so that it too isn't an eyesore.

Needless to say, the success of either configuration depends on some very complex acoustical issues, particularly reverberation and sound absorption—topics too complex for discussion here. If you know a good acoustician, ask him or her to evaluate your space before you do anything. This is especially true when selecting speakers. In the case of configuration one, for example, you will want speakers with good, wide dispersions that spread the sound evenly over a wide area. For configuration two, you may need speakers with more directionality, like the aforementioned columns.

As to the placement of speakers on stage for sound effects, the rule is to locate the speaker as close to where the sound is supposedly coming from. However, the audience cannot judge distance very well, so you can afford to be somewhat general. If we see someone on stage right looking out a window, listening to the sound of traffic, it is only necessary that the speaker be placed somewhere stage right; it does not have to be next to the window. Remember, however, to put the speaker on a pedestal or box, since it will lose its efficiency if it simply sits on the floor.

One final word: the ideal sound setup is unobtrusive, one of which the audience is unaware. That is the real trick.

34 | *Microphone Clinic*

*I*n the days of Ethel Merman and other "belters," musical performers didn't have to be miked. Singers then were trained to reach the last seat in the last row. In any case, they had to—microphone technology was not nearly what it is today and the cost of mics was far greater than it is today.

Today, of course, performers on Broadway are always miked, and performers in regional, academic, and community theater frequently are too. But while mics have brought great benefits with them, they also have created some problems.

Here's some general advice on how to take good care of your mics so they will take good care of you, and then some answers to a specific mic problem.

How to Maintain Your RF Wireless System

If your theater uses an RF wireless mic system, here is a collection of tips from the service staff at the Sennheiser microphone company that should help you maintain the longevity and performance of your mics and your system.

■ Never leave batteries installed for prolonged periods in either a transmitter or a receiver. If the batteries leak, you may find that the system will work only intermittently.

■ Standard distance between a sound source and a clip-on mic should be four to eight inches. Omnidirectional microphones generally yield the best results. They are free from proximity effects and exhibit little handling noise. (A proximity effect is an increase in bass heard from most directional microphones when you move them close to the sound source. Handling noise is the thump or click heard when a mic rubs against a surface.)

■ Ensure that the path between transmitter and receiver is relatively unobstructed.

■ If your particular theater does not require any or all receivers to be located backstage, try locating them physically closer to the stage where the actors will be performing. Running long audio lines is far preferable to long coaxial-cable runs.

■ When installing your microphone system, use the correct coaxial cable. RF signals are attenuated to different degrees in the various cable types. We recommend the use of quality RG-58/U-type cable for up to 25 feet, RG-8/X for 25 feet to approximately 50 feet, and RG/213/U or special low-loss broadcast cable (for instance, Belden Type 9913) beyond this distance.

■ The transmitting antenna should be spaced from the body of the actors as far as possible to minimize RF-absorption losses. Avoid direct body contact. Even 1/32 of an inch can make a dramatic difference.

■ If you are using VHF body-pack transmitters, do not use a stubby, flexible "Rubber Duck" antenna. The standard whip is more efficient and exhibits less degradation when close to the body. The Rubber Duck antenna should be used only with a receiver.

■ Active transmitters should not be placed closer than four inches to each other. Otherwise, signals may be picked up from the neighboring transmitter and intermodulation in the final stages may occur.

■ Compensate for receiving antenna cable and splitter losses greater than six decibels with suitable antenna boosters or active antennas.

■ To minimize the risk of intermodulation when using more than two channels, channels should be chosen from blocks of eight adjacent frequencies (for example, 1 through 8, 9 through 16, 17 through 24, or 25 through 32).

■ The minimum distance between the transmitter and receiver antenna should be no less than 16 feet to avoid receiver input overload and resulting intermodulation or desensitizing effects.

Sudden Static

What should you do when your wireless mics have static for no apparent reason—right in the middle of the big second act number scene? What could the problem possibly be?

Wireless mics are, by their very nature, tricky things and it's difficult (if not impossible) to be absolutely sure what might be causing static problems. But here are some tips that may help you avoid the problem or solve it when it crops up:

Change the batteries for every performance. Do it automatically, as most sound technicians do. If the static gets worse during the course of the performance, try changing the batteries at the intermission as well. Wireless mics can and do eat batteries.

Check out the connections between the transmitter pack and the mic element. You might have a dry joint in the plug or a loose plug. Also, try changing the mic element for a spare. You might have an intermittent break in the cable between the element and its plug. Also, the element could be bad. The element, lead, and plug are subject to enormous amounts of stress and strain, and are a common fault location.

Check out the aerial connection to the transmitter pack.

Check the aerial and audio connections to the receiver and from the receiver to your sound desk.

If you've tried moving the receiver higher up and that hasn't worked, try moving it closer to the stage as well. Try it actually *on* the stage. The shorter the distance from transmitter to receiver, the better.

Check out what the actor who wears the mic is wearing in the way of clothing or jewelry. Something like a large metal belt buckle next to the transmitter aerial is a possible source of static problems. So might be any clothing worn made out of nylon or anything else that builds up static charges or conducts electricity.

The static could be interference from something else. Does it coincide with heating or ventilation systems turning on in your building or a neighboring building? Any flickering fluorescent lights about? Faulty street lights outside, anything like that? Try switching on and off any other electrical equipment in the building.

Is anybody in a nearby building (or even the same building) using a transmitter, such as taxi companies, emergency services, or security guards?

Does the transmitter pack or mic element get soaked in the actor's sweat? If so, protect it.

If you can, try a completely different mic/transmitter pack/receiver/mixer channel combination. One or another item in the chain might be faulty.

Any or all of these could be the source of a static problem. To find that problem, you'll just have to go step by step, eliminating one by one the potential causes.

35 | *Since You Asked*
Body Mics and Book Voices

Q: Would you please explain the use of concealed body mics with details on component placement?

A: A body microphone (or "mic") is a type of concealed radio microphone that is connected to a pocket-sized transmitter also concealed on the performer. Signals are transmitted to a receiver usually located just off stage or in the control booth.

Because each mic transmits a separate signal, a sound technician must pay constant attention to the volume and quality of the sound from each. As with any electronic sound enhancement, the goal should be crisp, clear sound with no forced quality that would distract from the stage performance.

Body mics have made it much easier to provide uniform sound under otherwise adverse acoustical conditions. However, despite improvements in all components, radio microphones are still plagued by problems. Because mics cannot be checked often enough to eliminate these problems, professional companies often keep spare transmitters backstage—in some cases, one for each mic in use. Obviously, this is an expensive proposition, which is why we do not recommend body mics for smaller theater companies.

To get the most out of body mics, keep four things in mind.

First, do not use these mics on any material that generates static electricity. Clothes also can make unfortunate rustling noises against the microphone unless it is firmly fixed. Allow enough time to experiment with placement with each performer—in costume—during technical rehearsals.

Second, make sure the mic is placed as near the performer's mouth as possible. Unless otherwise specified, most radio microphones are omnidirectional, providing a kind of general pickup that can cope with all the performer's head movements. As long as the mic is near the source of sound, feedback should not be a problem. However, if the mic is positioned on the chest, for example, or buried under fabric, the technician will have to crank up the gain on the receiver for the actor to be heard. When the gain is turned up, the mic can pick up sound coming from the loudspeakers, and you will have a feedback problem.

Third, body mics need frequent cleaning to remove perspiration and makeup. A good way to clean them is to use a cotton swab moistened in pure alcohol or electronic component cleaner. However, check the instructions that come with your microphones before using any solvent.

Finally, avoid mics with switches. Control should always be with the technician—and even there, accidents can occur. We recall the story of one Broadway actress who left the stage for the ladies' room without turning off her switch. However, that was more than thirty-five years ago, and today's systems allow a technician to fade out the sound on an actor's exit. Mics also should be fitted with a "pre-fade listen" button so that the technician can listen to the channel before the performer goes on stage to be sure that all is well before allowing the audience to hear.

Q: What would be the best means to do the "book" voice for the musical *How to Succeed in Business Without Really Trying*? Have a live actor do the voice or have the voice on tape? Then, do you use one tape per scene or one tape for the entire show?

A: There are advantages and disadvantages to each approach. Probably the simplest option is to do the voice live. This need not be done by an actor who does only this, by the way; it could be handled by someone playing a smaller role, such as the chairman of the board, Mr. Womper, who doesn't appear until late in the show. From a technical standpoint, doing it live is easier because there's no tape to cue. However, where you place the microphone is crucial. The actor needs to be in plain sight of the person controlling the sound, or the stage manager, or on headsets, so he knows when to speak. Make sure the mic is out of the way of backstage traffic, and use a control panel or mixer to turn on the mic when needed; a switch on some mics makes an audible "thump" when activated.

If you have an actor with the perfect voice but who doesn't want to sit backstage and do the voiceovers, tape is the only alternative. We advise using one tape on a cassette deck with a real-time counter. The first cue begins at 01:00, then leave 15 seconds or so of blank tape before the second cue, and so on. (It also may help the sound technician if each cue starts on the minute—the second cue beginning at 02:00, the third at 03:00, and so on.) The blank space after each cue is there just in case someone forgets to stop the tape immediately when the voiceover is finished. Begin each cue with a second or two of silence as well, so you don't risk starting halfway into the first word of the speech.

If you don't have a tape deck with a real-time counter, you can cue up by listening to the tape through headphones with the house sound turned off (many tape decks have a headphone jack for this purpose).

Using multiple tapes means you have to keep track of them all. With everything on one tape, you simplify the process greatly, and can be confident that the sound cues are in the right order.

RESOURCES
Books and Video

We don't pretend that this book can answer every question or provide advice on every topic in musical theater. In fact, no one resource can do it all. That's why we've included this listing of books and videos that we think producers, directors, and performers will find particularly useful. (See also Part IV, "Musical Direction and Choreography" for musical resources.) Enjoy!

36 | "How Long Has This Been Going On?"

Help on the Printed Page, from A to Z

You'll find a wealth of books on musical theater in general, as well as on acting and directing. Here are a few that we have found particularly useful. Unless otherwise mentioned, all are available through your local or online bookseller.

American Musical Theatre: A Chronicle, by Gerald Bordman, is now in its third edition, and is still the best overall survey of the American musical stage. In chronological order, the shows get brief descriptions of plot, performers, creators, and critical reaction. Especially helpful, Bordman sprinkles in brief biographical information about major performers, composers, and lyricists. The new edition brings the work up to the 1990s, but also provides an appendix that describes heretofore-forgotten musicals from the 1870s to 1910. Three helpful indexes list shows and sources, songs, and people. This is a must-have reference for any musical-theater library. (ISBN 0-19-513074-X, Oxford University Press)

Art Isn't Easy: The Achievement of Stephen Sondheim, by Joanne Gordon, is simply the best book on this composer's work. Gordon writes perceptively, with uncanny insight into Sondheim and musical theater in general. She examines each Sondheim show in detail, paying careful attention to both music and lyrics, and always guiding the reader to an understanding of the show's essence. The book is must reading for anyone directing or performing in a Sondheim show. (ISBN 0-8093-1407-X, Southern Illinois University Press)

Breaking Through: From Rock to Opera—The Basic Technique of Voice, by Gloria Bennett, stems from the author's simple rule of thumb: "Does it hurt? Does it feel unnatural? Does it make you hoarse after long periods of singing? Then don't do it!" Her easy-to-follow guidebook includes techniques to improve and control the voice, placement and resonance, the natural range of the voice, vocal exercises, physical exercises, advanced technique, and case histories of various singers. She also explains how to use vocal exercises not only to warm up the voice, but also to help expand its range, and discusses various vocal problems and their remedies. Her commonsense approach is refreshing. (ISBN 0-7935-7238-X, Hal Leonard Publishing)

The Broadway Musical: A Critical and Musical Survey, by Joseph Swain, is an in-depth look at the music underlying this very American art form. Using more than 150 printed musical excerpts, Swain shows how particular musical solutions to dramatic problems have given what was once only a light, popular genre the formal complexity and emotional range that can encompass a wide variety of styles and materials. Swain also sheds light on the current Broadway scene, with good insight into its future direction. This is not a beginner's guide to musical theater; it is a work full of information and insight that will increase considerably your understanding and appreciation of musical theater. (ISBN 0-19-507482-3, Oxford University Press)

Broadway Musicals Show by Show, by Stanley Green and updated by Kay Green, a 386-page book, remains a useful reference for those seeking basic information about Broadway musicals. The title does not refer to a comprehensive listing of every musical ever produced, but to the book's chronological organization (1866–1996). Each show listed includes composer, lyricist, librettist, producer, director, chore-ographer, cast, songs, New York run, a brief synopsis and, in most cases, a photograph. This always has been a handy reference, partic-ularly with its indexes of titles, composers, lyricists, librettists, direc-tors, choreographers, cast members, and theaters. (ISBN 0-7935-3083-0, Hal Leonard Publishing)

A Century of Musicals in Black and White, by Bernard L. Peterson, Jr., is a one-volume encyclopedia of musical stage works by, about, or involving African Americans. Allen Woll's landmark *Black Musical Theatre* (Louisiana State University Press) took an historical approach. Peterson's book, on the other hand, is an A to Z, show-by-show listing of everything from touring shows of the late 1800s into the 1990s. For each listing, he includes all known essential informa-tion, including date, composer, lyricist, cast, synopsis, musical num-bers, and further references if available. Appendices include a chronology of shows; information sources; and indexes of names, songs, and general information. This is an outstanding reference work. (ISBN 0-313-26657-3, Greenwood Press)

Conversations with Choreographers, by Svetlana McLee Grody and Dorothy Daniels Lister, is basically a series of question-and-answer interviews (conducted over the past twenty years), in which the authors explore the creative process of choreography with Hermes Pan, Donald Saddler, Ernest O. Flatt, Joe Layton, Ron Field, Michael Bennett, Bob Avian, Patricia Birch, Tommy Tune, Graciela Daniele, Wayne Cilento, and others. The result is candid and informative, and often highly entertaining. If you've thought of choreography as "doing the steps," this book will be a revelation. (ISBN 0-435-08697-9, Heinemann)

Enchanted Evenings: The Broadway Musical from Show Boat to Sondheim, by Geoffrey Block, provides an historical look at the American musical from 1927's *Show Boat* to the present. Using fourteen landmark shows as examples, Block focuses on the music, using original manuscript materials to show how composer, lyricist, librettist, and director work together to create a production. About one-quarter of the book is devoted to a complete discography, plot synopses, and song-by-song scenic outlines for each of the fourteen shows. For those wanting a more in-depth look at the art of the American musical, this book will be an eye-opener. (ISBN 0-19-510791-8, Oxford University Press)

From *Assassins to West Side Story*, by Scott Miller, focuses on an issue facing many directors. As more theater companies and schools produce shows like *Assassins* and *Sweeney Todd*, a different approach is needed. While this could be classified as a how-to book, Miller doesn't really tell others how to direct these more complex shows. Instead, he offers suggestions on how to conceptualize a musical by finding its textual and musical themes, as well as exploring the more fully developed characters of such musicals as *Gypsy* and *Company*, understanding the historical and social context of the action, and determining the creators' intentions. To do this, each chapter focuses on one musical and dissects it with great insight and skill. Once you see how Miller does this, you can use the same technique on any musical that warrants this sort of in-depth approach. His take on *Into the Woods* is especially fine, but the entire book is well done and eminently readable. (ISBN 0-435-08699-5, Heinemann)

The Great Song Thesaurus, by Roger Lax and Frederick Smith, lists what the publishers claim is "virtually every [popular] song written in the last four hundred years." The 774-page volume includes the most popular and distinguished songs listed by year of popularity (up through 1987); songs from theater scores and musical and non-musical films, television, and radio; British and American award-winning songs; entertainers' and performers' themes, trademarks, and signature songs; advertising jingles; song plagiarism, adaptations, and revivals; college and university songs; political campaign songs; church chimes and carillons; and American bugle calls. The most useful portion (and what the book title seems to be about) is a listing of 2,300 song titles by subject, key word, and category. There's a lot of information here for directors or sound technicians who are trying to locate the right song for a particular dramatic moment. (ISBN 0-19-505408-3, Oxford University Press)

How to Audition for the Musical Theatre, by Donald Oliver, is a step-by-step guide aimed primarily at professional performers, although most of the information will be useful to anyone who works in musical theater. Oliver explains the audition process, including the production team that does the casting and the interactive elements of the process. He explains how to arrange a professional audition and work with agents and casting directors. The heart of the book is the information on preparation and performing. Oliver discusses where to find an accompanist, how to build a repertoire of songs (including what not to sing), and where to find songs. He explains interpreting the song, working with a vocal coach, and the mechanics of a good audition. He includes appendices on "overdone, uninspired (and inappropriate) audition songs," resumés and photos, the pros and cons of using an agent, and a list of helpful names and addresses. (ISBN 1-880399-58-X, Smith and Kraus)

How to Direct a Musical, by David Young, explains how directing a musical is much different than a straight play, full of pitfalls that can try the patience of Job. An experienced director and professor, Young makes good use of excerpts from a diary he kept while directing a production of the musical Fanny, including why and how decisions (right and wrong) were made. He also discusses issues and tasks to be undertaken before rehearsals begin, auditions and casting, first rehearsals, working on acting with singers and dancers, working with an orchestra and choreographer, production numbers, and much more. Topics include basics as well as more advanced work, and there are lots of photos, staging diagrams, exercises, and special notes on key but often overlooked points. (ISBN 0-87830-052-X, Routledge)

Let's Put on a Musical, by Peter Filichia, is a wonderful resource. Musicals are grouped by common threads—showcases for your finest performer, shows for predominantly male and female casts, choices for grade school and junior high school, for high schools, and shows that don't depend on young casts. Filichia highlights musicals that rely heavily on costumes and those that don't, musicals for musicians who can act, cult shows that haven't found their audience, and holiday and ethnic musicals. (ISBN 0-8230-8817-0, Back Stage Books)

Musical: A Grand Tour, by Denny Martin Flinn, attempts nothing less than a history of the art and craft of the American musical from its Greco-Roman roots to modern Broadway. That's a tall order for 556 pages, but Flinn is surprisingly successful, and it makes for enjoyable reading. The first eighty pages cover the history of musical theater before *The Black Crook,* the first acknowledged American musical comedy (1866). Flinn then alternates between discussions of genres (revue, operetta, the Princess musicals), innovators (George M. Cohan, Agnes de Mille, Jerome Robbins), and the basic building blocks of book, lyrics, and music. Those who think of musical theater in terms of composers and lyricists may find Flinn's approach unusual, even heretical. However, the book's focus also provides a refreshingly different viewpoint. (ISBN 0-02-864610-X, Schirmer Books)

Musicals: Directing School and Community Theatre, by Robert Boland and Paul Argentini, is essentially a how-to manual for those new to musical production. The authors explain how a director prepares, rehearses, and produces a musical. Step by step, they take the reader through selecting a show, obtaining the script, and signing the contract; auditions; casting; developing the rehearsal schedule; choreography; publicity; box office; opening night; and strike. Illustrations, charts, and photographs are included, as well as a bibliography and glossary. As might be expected in such a book, some subjects (such as lighting and set design) do not get in-depth treatment, but the authors do cover basic fundamentals. In particular, we applaud the focus on the preparation of the director's prompt book, an invaluable tool that facilitates the entire process of rehearsals, staging, and blocking. (ISBN 0-8108-3323-9, Scarecrow Press)

Next! Auditioning for the Musical Theatre, by Steven M. Alper, covers music preparation, working with an accompanist, what to sing and what not to sing, and the mechanics of the audition. In fact, the section on accompanists is almost worth the price of the book. (Alper is an audition accompanist as well as a composer and musical director.) Alper's first-hand observations are always right on the mark. (ISBN 0-435-08686-3, Heinemann)

Not Since Carrie: 40 Years of Broadway Musical Flops, by Ken Mandelbaum, is both fascinating and fun. We read of fascinating failure after failure, with much good inside information about why the show failed, and even the good things that might make one consider reviving some of them. This last point will be its main attraction to readers of this book. After all, there are many lesser known (or unknown) musicals listed in various publishers' catalogues, but how good are they? If they appeared on Broadway (or were headed there), Mandelbaum discusses them, often with keen insight. For example, describing *Baby,* the 1983 failure about having babies (what else?), Mandelbaum calls it "a perfect piece for community theater and stock productions, with an outstanding score, one of the best heard on Broadway in the eighties." And of *70 Girls, 70,* he notes that while the show ran only a brief time, "It deserved to be a success—it played as well or as better than many a hit—and did not merit the barrage of critical disapproval that deprived it of ever finding an audience. *70 Girls, 70* is ideal material for groups with older performers, and its production demands are minimal." Due to the amount of material, Mandelbaum has to keep his descriptions short, often when you wish he'd stop and tell more. Still, this is a reference book that will be consulted again and again, because many of the shows aren't described at length in any other book. (ISBN 0-312-06428-4, St. Martin's Press)

Rodgers and Hammerstein, by Ethan Mordden, is a coffee-table book that actually has something valuable to say about these two. As always, Mordden goes beyond historical record and personal anecdote to share with the reader his own particular viewpoint. While this is a wonderful browser's book, it also would make excellent reading for anyone about to direct one of the R&H shows. Of particular note are the comparisons of stage production with the film versions, and the incisive analysis of the team's three flops, *Allegro, Me and Juliet,* and *Pipe Dream.* (ISBN 0-8109-1567-7, Harry N. Abrams, Inc.)

Show Tunes by Steven Suskin is subtitled "The Songs, Shows, and Careers of Broadway's Major Composers." The book is organized by composer, with an annotated listing of each show, where it was first performed, length of run, performers, and a brief description. Although this information can be found in some other volumes, Suskin's is more complete than most and well organized. What sets it apart, however, is the listing of songs from each show, divided into "published songs," "additional songs published in vocal score," "recorded songs," "additional recorded songs," etc. Suskin doesn't give the name of the publisher or recording company, but at least it gives the reader a place to start looking. I used the book the second day I had it when a friend called up to ask whether the song "Distant Melody" from *Peter Pan* was ever published. According to Suskin, it was, so the friend could start her search. (ISBN 0-19-512599-1, Oxford University Press)

Singing Professionally: Studying Singing for Actors and Singers, by Arabella Hong Young, is a much-needed addition to the library of the musical-theater performer. Young begins with basic foundations for voice production and continues through techniques of fully developed singing. Her approach is her own, by combining a variety of classical vocal techniques and adapting them for musical theater. It is difficult to convey this sort of content in written form, but Young (a veteran of the Broadway and concert stage) makes her points clearly, aided by helpful illustrations and a page design that separates and underscores individual concepts. Topics covered include breath support (surely the most essential skill for any musical performer other than staying on pitch), voice placement, vocal range, how to practice, working with different registers, dealing with high notes, and a number of advanced techniques such as coloratura, falsetto, and acting while singing. This is certainly one of the best books on this subject that we have seen. Young is to be congratulated for presenting this information in clear, straightforward fashion. It's a reference that performers will use again and again. Our highest recommendation. (ISBN 0-435-08677-4, Heinemann)

Staging Musical Theatre, by Elaine A. Novak and Deborah Novak, calls itself the "complete guide for directors, choreographers, and producers"—and lives up to its billing, with fifteen well-written chapters that cover every important issue and task. Because this book is designed for those new to staging musical productions, the authors provide some scenes for practice, plus an annotated list of large- and small-scale musicals. (ISBN 1-55870-407-8, Betterway Publications)

Writing the Broadway Musical, by Aaron Frankel, explores in detail the creation of book, music, and lyrics. This could be read as a how-to book by the aspiring musical writer. On the other hand, it could be used as a classroom text or personal reference book in its ability to explain the process of how a musical is put together. (ISBN 0-306-80943-5, Da Capo Press)

"I Can See It" 37
Video Instruction for the Director and Actor

Born to Sing touches every aspect from basics to advanced. The authors explain, demonstrate everything well, and have you exercise with them. Primarily aimed at beginners, there is still value here for those who have had some vocal instruction and wish to use the video as an aid for practice. In addition to the video, there is a series of tapes and CDs. (Music World/Vocal Power; 800/929-SING; or online at <www.borntosing.com>)

Movement for the Actor benefits from the solid presentation by Dawn Mora, with the help of Northwestern University students. Not specifically aimed at musical theater, Mora's video explains preparatory issues such as stretching and basic technique, as well as the use of gesture and movement to underscore character and text. (First Light Video; 800/262-8862; or online at <www.firstsightvideo.com>)

Music Theatre International's *Conversationpiece* series presents background information about individual musicals of great use to directors, cast, designers, and theater students. For example, *Into the Woods* features a discussion by bookwriter and director James Lapine and composer/lyricist Stephen Sondheim. The *She Loves Me* video features composer Jerry Bock, lyricist Sheldon Harnick, and bookwriter Joe Masteroff. Other *Conversationpiece* videos include *Baby*, with creators David Shire, Richard Maltby, Jr., and Roger Englander; and *Once on This Island*, with librettist Lynn Ahrens, composer Stephen Flaherty, and director/choreographer Graciela Daniele. Also in the series are *Assassins*, *Forever Plaid*, and *The World Goes Round*. A single copy of *The Video Conversationpiece* is provided for your licensed Music Theatre International show. The company also offers a free multi-title sampler for your perusal. (421 W. 54th St., New York, NY 10019; 212/541-4684; or online at <www.mtishows.com>)

Step by Step: An Amateur's Video Guide to Choreography, is a 60-minute production packed with helpful ideas in an entertaining format. Part I gives you fundamental techniques; Part II discusses and demonstrates basic choreographed moves.

Part III offers explanations and presentations of basic steps. We found this particularly useful—to have these sometimes familiar steps given a name and then broken down into their component parts. We suspect you'll run this part again and again as you take notes or try out the steps yourself. Part IV is on stylization—those elements that give polish to the performance. It starts with combinations of basic steps, then shows you how to stylize them for different settings—western, urban sophisticated, gangster, sailor, military, and so on. You'll also learn how to make good use of props, and develop professional bows and curtseys. This latter point is more important than you think—the bow is the last element the audience is likely to remember about your show. We like this video because it explains dance in the context of the show, including the elements of character and plot. That's an element that is often overlooked. It also uses "real" people as examples, not Broadway performers. (Pioneer Drama Service; P.O. Box 4267, Englewood, CO 80155-4267; 800/333-7262; or online at <www .pioneerdrama.com>)

Voice Workout for the Actor is a bit mistitled, since it actually is a 30-minute whole-body workout, including exercises for relaxing and stretching, face preparation, and pitch and resonance, as well as tongue twisters. Unlike aerobic-exercise tapes, this one is appropriately low-key and relaxing because it is meant to prepare—not tire—the actor for performance. In her introduction, Susan Leigh advises that when you use the tape repeatedly, you fast-forward to the start of the exercises, turn the sound down, and use your favorite music while you keep your eye on what's going on on-screen. (ISBN 1-883779-00-6; Theatre Arts Video Library; or online at <www.members.aol.com/tavlvideo>)

Final Words

*T*o put on a musical, you need—as we have indicated many times in the preceding pages—a multiplicity of skills. In fact, the skill probably most in demand for a director, musical director, performer, or anyone involved in musical theater might very well be the skill of juggling different skills.

That is, during the production process, different situations will demand different approaches; different times will require different insights. You need to remain flexible and you need to be adaptable. You must see the small details and the big picture.

It's a lot of work, of course. But when all the parts coalesce and all the skills have been brought to the fore, magic can happen. It's important to remember that as well.

Maybe the hapless Washington Senators, in *Damn Yankees*, put it best:

You gotta have heart.
Miles and miles and miles of heart.
When the odds are saying you'll never win,
That's when the grin should start.

Contributors

Malcolm Bowes teaches at Indiana University of Pennsylvania.

Hope S. Breslauer is a former editor at *Stage Directions*.

Mike Bromberg is a regular contributor to *Stage Directions*. He is an electronic design engineer who designs lighting principally for light opera in the New England area.

Scott Miller is the artistic director of New Line Theatre in St. Louis.

Stephen Peithman, the founding Editor of *Stage Directions*, is currently Consulting Editor at the magazine.

Nancianne Pfister, former Associate Editor of *Stage Directions*, teaches at American River College in Sacramento, California.

Diane Seymour is a founding member of The Actors Institute in New York City and a playwright and lyricist.

Lisa Viall is the librarian at the Goodspeed Opera Library of Musical Theatre.

MORE BOOKS

from Heinemann's *Stage Directions* series
Stephen Peithman and Neil Offen, *Editors*

Stage Directions Guide to Working Back Stage

The *Stage Directions Guide to Working Back Stage* focuses on how to create a truly collaborative and supportive back-stage effort, with information on: proper installation and maintenance of rope, rigging, and curtains; safety guidelines for ladders, catwalks, and other high places; use, clean-up, and storage of paints and adhesives; and more.

0-325-00244-4 / 176pp / 2000

Stage Directions Guide to Shakespeare

Contained in this volume is practical advice on everything a regional, community, or academic theater needs to know when taking the plunge into a Shakespearean play, including reasons to do (or not to do) Shakespeare.

0-325-00233-9 / 112pp / 2000

Stage Directions Guide to Publicity

If your theater isn't on Broadway and doesn't have an expensive press agent (or ad budget), how does it get attention? That's where this book steps in, providing information on what draws an audience to a show, how to improve your mail pieces, tips for more effective ads, and other aspects of the publicity game.

0-325-00082-4 / 114pp / 1999

Stage Directions Guide to Auditions

This book offers expert advice on a range of audition topics, including choosing the right monologue, preparing your voice for auditions, steps to getting cast, sealing the deal at callbacks, and more.

0-325-00083-2 / 144pp / 1998

Stage Directions Guide to Directing

All directors—from beginners to the most experienced—will find in this book invaluable information to make their direction more effective. Topics include things to look for in an audition, selecting the right play, criticizing effectively, basics of directing a musical, and more!

0-325-00112-X / 168pp / 1999

Stage Directions Guide to Getting and Keeping Your Audience

How does a theater attract and maintain the audience it needs? You'll find out how in this book, discovering practical suggestions on advertising to motivate ticket-buyers, creating attention-getting mailings, and more!

0-325-00113-8 / 148pp / 1999

For more information about these books, visit us online at **www.heinemanndrama.com**, call **800-225-5800**, fax **203-750-9790**, or write: Heinemann, Promotions Dept., 361 Hanover St., Portsmouth, NH 03801.